Hamlyn all-colour paperbacks

John Davies

Sailing

illustrated by Bill Stallion

Hamlyn · London
Sun Books · Melbourne

FOREWORD

We are living in a new Elizabethan age as far as adventurous
voyages under sail are concerned. Brave men cross oceans and
even circle the world in small vessels, often single-handed. Trans-
atlantic races, and others such as the New York–Bermuda and
Sydney–Hobart races are established features of the international
calendar.

The people who go in for this sort of sailing derive their own
satisfaction from it. At the other end of the scale there are thousands
of men, women and children who get just as much fulfilment, and
sometimes as much excitement, out of 'voyages' which never take
them out of sight of land – or even of the clubhouse. And between
these two extremes there are all sorts of degrees of competence and
performance.

Competence and performance: these are important words, words to
be remembered by anybody who is starting to sail – and, indeed,
by those who are sailing already. Sailing is different from most
other sports in that it is *dangerous*.

This statement is not made to frighten you, nor to dampen your
enthusiasm. It is a plain statement of fact. As I have emphasized
later in this book, the sea (or a river, or a lake) *can drown you*.

To put it another way, it is vital that you should never do more, or
venture further, than your experience at the time will safely permit.

This book is intended to teach the fundamentals of the sport.
And the emphasis throughout is on safety.

*N.B. There are no sail numbers in the illustrations in this book because
representative rather than specific craft are shown.*

Published by The Hamlyn Publishing Group Ltd
London · New York · Sydney · Toronto
Hamlyn House, Feltham, Middlesex, England
In association with Sun Books Pty. Ltd. Melbourne.

SBN 600001105
Phototypeset by BAS Printers Limited, Wallop, Hampshire
Colour separations by Schwitter Limited, Zurich
Printed in England by Sir Joseph Causton & Sons Limited

CONTENTS

Yachting yesterday : boats like the big J class yachts seen here needed paid crews to handle and maintain them. Only rich men could indulge in this form of sport.

BOATS . . . BOATS . . . AND YET MORE BOATS

Sailing has developed more sensationally in recent years than any other sport. Before the last war it was essentially a rich man's diversion, and was called 'yachting'. Since then there has been a tremendous proliferation of sailing craft and of new designs, materials and methods of construction; and this expansion is still continuing.

The world of 'yachting', which conjures up pictures of gentlemen in white-topped caps and reefer jackets (and paid crews to do the hard and dirty work) has virtually disappeared. In its place we have another picture, of men, women and children of all sorts and conditions 'messing about in boats', not only at every practicable point around our coasts, but in rivers and creeks, and even on reservoirs and flooded gravel pits. They do their own maintenance, sail their boats themselves, and even build them, from do-it-yourself kits, which are cheap and easy to build.

Dinghies by the dozen . . .

. . . by the score, the hundred, the thousand! The sailing explosion has naturally been the most dramatic where these small boats are concerned, because they are the cheapest of all sailing craft to buy and maintain, and also the most convenient – a dinghy can be sailed on pretty well any handy bit of water. You do not have to find a mooring. You can keep your boat at home, which is convenient for maintenance, and when you want to sail, you just hook her on the back of your car and away you go.

Most modern dinghies belong to a class, and you can see how these classes have grown just by glancing at their sails. The mainsails of 'class' dinghies carry a letter or symbol denoting the class, together with the serial number. Some of these numbers are now well up in the thousands.

Sailing today : the great sailing explosion of post-war years has been chiefly in the dinghy field: There are now many different dinghy classes, with thousands of boats in some of them. In the foreground below are examples of two of the most popular classes – an Enterprise (*left*) and a Mirror.

Pocket cruisers

There has also been a great increase in the number of small cabin boats on the market, and a marked improvement in their performance and accommodation. As a result of this, there is nowadays a good choice of boats of not much more than dinghy size, aboard which two people can live, for short periods at least, in some degree of comfort.

If these little cruisers are properly designed, built and equipped, they will be perfectly safe and seaworthy. A word of warning here, though. An important consideration affecting the safety of small boats at sea is the fitness and experience of the people aboard. It is what the crew, rather than the boat, is capable of that should be the limiting factor in any venture.

Two modestly-priced little cruisers suitable for the beginner are the two-berth Silhouette and the four-berth Westerly. Both these boats can be trailed.

Learning the ropes

So far we have been talking about owning your own boat, but in fact most people 'learn the ropes' aboard someone else's craft – a friend's, or perhaps a club boat. Some go to sailing schools. If the school is a good one, these people will start very much on the right track, because they will be taught by a qualified instructor.

Boats for hire

Some people receive some of their earlier experience by hiring ('chartering') boats. There are now many excellent charter firms to choose from, and most of them advertise in the sailing press.

It is much easier to charter a boat now than it was a few years ago, and on the whole charter boats are much better than they used to be. The picture shows typical small sailing cruisers operated by a charter firm.

Two popular small cruisers. The one above is a Westerly 22, a bilge-keeled glass fibre boat with room for four people. There are larger Westerlys as well. Below is a Signet 20, a similar type of boat, but this time from America.

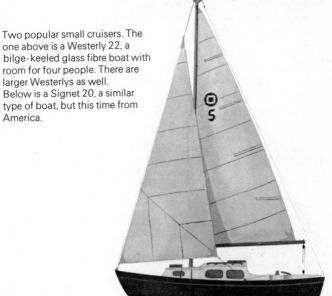

Coastal or inland waters?

Whether you sail on the sea or on a river or lake will depend in most cases on where you live and what sort of sailing you want to do. If you do not live within reasonably easy reach

Racing is very popular, because it gives an added purpose to sailing, and takes the measure of one's skill...
... but it is pleasant to potter about at times, even in a boat which is designed primarily for racing.

of a suitable stretch of coast, sea sailing will be difficult for you; and in Britain at least, cruising probably will be too, since there are only a few inland sailing areas extensive enough to make this form of sport possible. The most notable of these areas are the networks of rivers and meres in Norfolk and Suffolk known as the Broads. These waters are a Mecca of the charter business, and thousands of people gain their first sailing experience here in hired craft.

Some waters may be described as 'semi-open sea', and these are perhaps the most suitable of all for the ordinary small-boat sailor. In Britain, such waters are the Solent, the river-estuary-coast complex of Essex and Suffolk, and the Clyde. On the eastern seaboard of the USA there are many hundreds of miles of safe sailing of this kind, in particular in Long Island Sound.

To race – or not to race ?

If your craft is a dinghy, two kinds of sailing are open to you. You can potter about, or you can race. On restricted inland waters, racing is very much the order of the day, and for a very good reason. There is a limit to how much pottering you can do without becoming bored. Racing adds purpose, and the element of competition.

If you have a dinghy and sail it on the sea, the opportunities for pottering will obviously be greater. But even on the sea the same limitations apply, if to a lesser degree, and most dinghy sailors are bitten by the racing bug sooner or later.

If you have a cabin boat, the chances are that (to start with, at any rate) you will spend most of your time cruising, with perhaps an occasional race, just for the fun of it. You can always graduate later to ocean racing!

This is perhaps a suitable place to say something about sailing clubs. There has been a proliferation of such clubs in recent years, especially for dinghy sailors. Most of them are quite modest affairs, but they all provide the basics of competition and good company.

Whatever kind of sailing you go in for, it is important that you should know what you are doing right from the beginning. It is with these vital 'first steps' that this little book will be chiefly concerned.

Moving under sail

Let us start by seeing how a sailing vessel converts her fuel (the wind) into movement; what the restrictions on this movement are, and how sailing craft have developed towards a more and more effective use of their motive power.

Rig

'Rig' means, fundamentally, the way a vessel's sails are presented to the wind.

Square rig was the most elementary form of the above. A square-rigged vessel has her sails (or her major sails) set athwartships, that is, across the vessel.

The 'long ships' of the Vikings were good examples of simple square rig. These vessels sailed well if they had a favourable wind, which meant one coming from somewhere astern. If it was blowing from ahead, the Norsemen had to row.

The large sailing ships of the great days of sail were basically square-rigged. Improvements resulting from centuries of experience gave them much better performance against the wind than the earliest square-riggers, but they were still severely limited in this respect.

With **fore-and-aft rig**, the sails can be so angled that they will catch not only a wind coming from astern or on the beam (at right-angles to the vessel) but also one blowing from somewhere ahead (diagonally ahead; no vessel will sail against a wind coming from directly ahead).

With this rig, the forward edges of the sails are made fast to the spars or rigging of the vessel, and the angle of their presentation to the wind is controlled by ropes attached to their after corners. With a wind coming from diagonally ahead, the sails have to be hauled in until they are more or less parallel to the fore-and-aft (front-to-back) line of the vessel. Hence the name of the rig.

One of the most important aspects of fore-and-aft rig is the balance of the sail plan. The total action of the wind on the sails should be such that the boat will steer easily under all conditions. If the balance is incorrect, it may be hard work to prevent her heading into or turning away from the wind. Nowadays, all small sailing craft are fore-and-aft rigged.

10

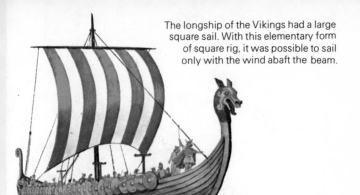

The longship of the Vikings had a large square sail. With this elementary form of square rig, it was possible to sail only with the wind abaft the beam.

The feluccas and dhows of Middle Eastern waters anticipated the modern yacht's fore-and-aft rig by thousands of years. These vessels can sail against the wind as well as before it.

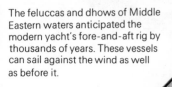

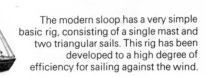

The modern sloop has a very simple basic rig, consisting of a single mast and two triangular sails. This rig has been developed to a high degree of efficiency for sailing against the wind.

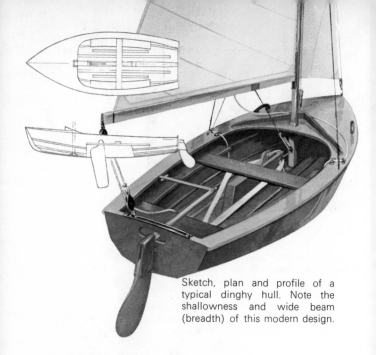

Sketch, plan and profile of a typical dinghy hull. Note the shallowness and wide beam (breadth) of this modern design.

PARTS OF A SAILING BOAT
The hull

Let us first look at a few 'technical terms':—

The **bow** is the front, or 'sharp' end.

The **stern** is the rear, or after end.

The width of the boat at its widest point is its **beam**.

A boat's greatest depth in the water is its **draught**.

The **keel** is, properly, the main fore-and-aft member on which the framework of a boat is constructed, but the term is popularly used to refer to the projection from the bottom of the boat which helps to prevent her being pushed sideways by the wind and, in some cases, from capsizing.

Hull design

Half a century ago, sailing craft tended to be much narrower than they are now, and have, generally speaking, considerably deeper draught. The idea was that a narrow boat would cut through the water better, while the deep draught would give her a better 'grip' and more stability. Since then boats have increased in beam and decreased in draught. For a number of years normal beam was considered to be roughly one third of the waterline length, but recently there has been a marked increase in beam beyond this (American designers have led the way here). The modern boat tends to be broad-beamed and of shallow draught. Such boats are 'drier' than old designs, that is, instead of cutting through the water, throwing it up over the bows, they ride over the waves and keep the crew dry.

Another major change (applying to cruising boats, not dinghies) is in the relationship of the boat's waterline length to her length at deck level. In 'old-timers' there was very little difference between these two dimensions, whereas the average modern boat is considerably shorter on the water-line. This is another factor which goes towards making a boat 'dry', and it also makes her more manoeuvrable.

Sketch, plan and profile of a typical small (two berth) sailing cruiser. This craft has twin bilge-keels (see page 14).

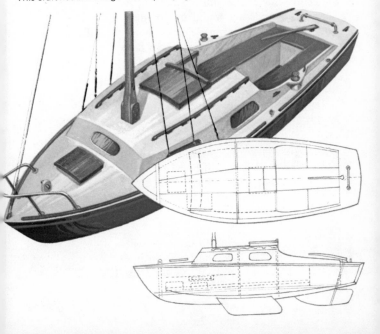

The Keel

For our purposes here, we will assume that the keel is that part of a sailing boat which projects below the hull.

Keels are of two main kinds, retractable and fixed.

Retractable keels

These, as their description indicates, are keels which can be raised or lowered as required.

Why **retractable**? It is an advantage to be able to raise the keel, either partly or completely, when the boat is sailing on such a course that the sideways thrust of the wind is either reduced or (when sailing with the wind due astern) eliminated. Raising the keel reduces the boat's 'drag' through the water, and her speed is increased. This applies particularly to dinghy sailing.

If the lowered keel touches bottom, it can be temporarily raised, to avoid the boat going aground.

It is obviously useful, too, when launching, beaching or trailing a boat.

There are two main kinds of **retractable keel**: centreboards and dagger boards. Both work through a trunking on the centre-line of the hull.

Centreboards are found in dinghies and a few cruising boats. They are either made of metal, or are ballasted so that they can be lowered under their own weight. They are pivoted at the forward end, and are so designed that they can be raised or lowered by a small tackle or other device inside the boat.

Dagger boards are found only in dinghies, and are much simpler than centreboards. They are just boards (not necess-

Types of keel : illustrated (*left to right*) are the two kinds of retractable keel (centreboard and dagger board) ; a boat with twin bilge keels ; a typical, 'faired-in' fixed keel ; and a fin keel.

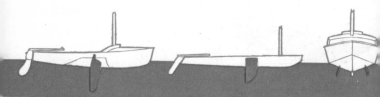

arily of wood) which are pushed down and pulled up directly by hand through a straight trunking.

Fixed keels

These are normally a feature of cabin boats; the most common kind consists of a shaped weight (of iron or lead) which is faired into the boat's general underwater profile.

A minority of boats have **fin keels**. As the term suggests, a fin keel projects like a fin from the underside of the hull.

One drawback of the two above kinds of keel is that when aground or ashore the boat will lie over on her side unless she is supported in some way. This is one reason why some boats have **bilge keels**.

Bilge keels run along the boat's bottom on either side of and parallel to a shallow, often only rudimentary central keel. They enable a boat to sit upright when out of the water, or in too little water to float – a great advantage should one, deliberately or accidentally, 'take the ground'.

What keels are for

All keels have one function in common, namely to prevent the boat being blown sideways and to help the helmsman steer the boat on as accurate a course as possible in all conditions of wind and current. In addition, most fixed keels (more properly called ballast keels because of their weight) give a boat stability by exerting a righting force against the capsizing force of the wind. Centreboards provide less stability, and dagger boards none at all, but this is compensated for in other ways, depending on the size of the boat, by extra beam and/or the righting factor provided by the suitable disposition of the weight of the person or persons sailing in the boat.

Spars and standing rigging

Spars

The spars of a boat are the 'poles' which support and extend the sails. Most modern sailing craft have two main spars:
The **mast** is the spar on which the sails are hoisted; the **boom** (main, or mainsail boom) is the spar along the bottom of the mainsail, which serves to stretch out the foot of the sail.

Many boats, especially those which race, also have a **spinnaker boom**, a light pole which is used to extend the foot of the 'balloon' sail called a spinnaker.

What spars are made of

The spars of a sailing craft may be made of wood, light metal alloy, or glass fibre. Wooden spars may be solid or hollow.

The spars and standing rigging of a modern sloop: the left-hand picture shows the two spars (mast and mainsail boom), shrouds, forestay and backstay. The bows-on illustration shows an alternative shroud-pattern, with only one set of spreaders.

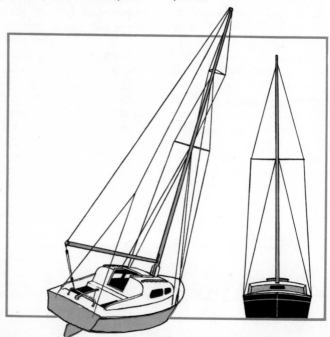

An old-timer's rigging : note the additional spars (gaff and bowsprit).

Alloy spars are much favoured nowadays because they are (a) stronger for a given weight than wooden spars, (b) more durable and (c) they require less maintenance. Glass fibre spars are also coming to the fore.

Standing rigging

By standing rigging, we mean the stays by which the mast or masts of the boat are supported. They are normally made of galvanized or stainless wire rope. In its simplest form standing rigging consists of the following stays:

the **forestay**, a wire stay stretching from the top or upper part of the mast to the bow of the boat;

the **backstay**, a wire stay stretching from the top of the mast to the stern of the boat.

These two stays give the mast fore-and-aft support.

Shrouds give a mast lateral support. They stretch from the sides of the boat abreast the mast to the top of the mast. There may be more than one on each side.

Sails

Most modern sailing craft have two basic sails – a small one in front of the mast, and a larger one behind it. The sail in front of the mast is the **jib**. The sail behind the mast is the **mainsail**.

Both these sails are triangular. Their sides and corners are named as follows:

The forward side or edge of the sail is the **luff**.

The after side is the **leech**.

The bottom side is the **foot**.

The top corner is the **head**.

The bottom forward corner is the **tack**.

The bottom after corner is the **clew**.

The luff of the jib is stretched taut between the bow of the boat and a point at or near the top of the mast. It is usually attached to the forestay by spring clips.

Nowadays the luff of the mainsail is usually attached to the after side of the mast by slides which work up and down a track on the mast. When the mainsail is hoisted, the luff is stretched taut.

The foot of the mainsail is often attached to the boom in the same way as it is to the mast, that is, by slides working along a track, although slides are not so important here because it is not normally necessary to adjust the foot of the mainsail while actually sailing, whereas the sail may have to be lowered or hoisted at any time.

The above two sails are the boat's normal or 'working' rig. She may have other sails as well.

Spinnaker

This is the balloon sail mentioned earlier, a three-cornered, light-weather sail which may be hoisted in front of the mast when the wind is coming from astern or from the beam.

Staysail (Genoa)

The staysail, sometimes called a Genoa, is another large tri-angular sail which may be hoisted in front of the mast when conditions permit. It is a large sail, sometimes as big as or even bigger than the mainsail.

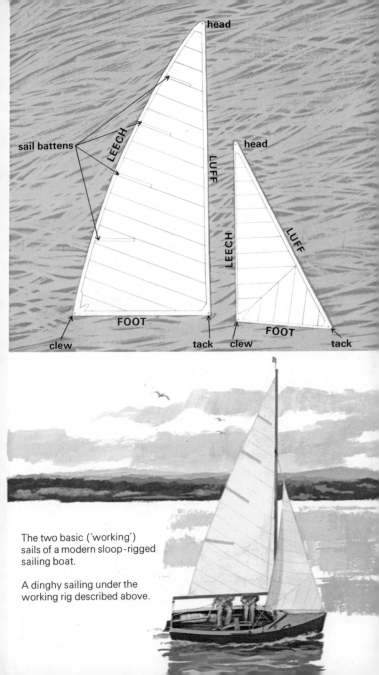

sail battens

LEECH

LUFF

head

LEECH

LUFF

head

FOOT

FOOT

clew

tack

clew

tack

The two basic ('working')
sails of a modern sloop-rigged
sailing boat.

A dinghy sailing under the
working rig described above.

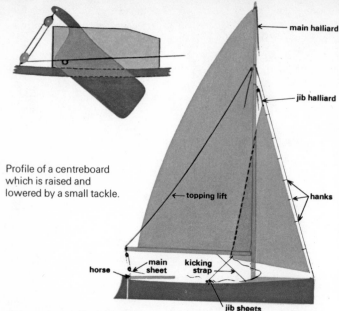

Profile of a centreboard which is raised and lowered by a small tackle.

A sloop-rigged dinghy, with her running rigging, including main and jib halliards; topping lift, supporting the end of the boom; jib-sheets, and mainsheet (with tackle).

Running rigging

By running rigging we mean the wires and ropes by which a boat's sails are hoisted and controlled.

Halliards

The ropes or wires by which a boat's sails are hoisted are called halliards (haul-yards), also spelt 'halyards'. Each

Rope control: (1) a jamming cleat; (2) a spring hook; (3) a shackle; (4) a sailing 'horse' along which the mainsheet travels.

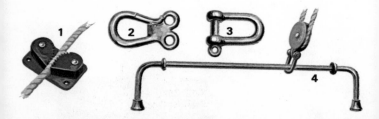

halliard is further identified by reference to the sail it hoists. Thus the mainsail is hoisted by the mainsail halliard, or main halliard, the jib by the jib halliard, and so on.

A halliard has to take a great deal of strain and must not have much 'give', since this would result in a slack luff. Halliards are therefore usually made of wire, with rope 'tails' (ends) for making them fast.

Sheets

These are the ropes controlling the angle at which the sails are presented to the wind. Like halliards, sheets are identified by reference to the sails which they control. Thus the mainsail is controlled by the mainsail sheet (usually called the mainsheet), the jib by jib sheets, and so on.

For ease of handling, and because they do not have to be set up taut like halliards, sheets are made of rope.

The sheets are attached to the clews (after corners) of sails forward of the mast, and to the after end of the mainsail boom. Any sail forward of the mast has to have two sheets so that the sail can be controlled on either side of the mast. In the case of the mainsail the mast is not an obstruction, so this sail can be controlled by a single sheet. We therefore speak of a boat's mainsheet in the singular, but of her jib or staysail sheets in the plural.

Materials

Until quite recently 'natural' rope (hemp etc.) was used for sheets, but Terylene and other synthetic ropes are now coming very much to the fore. These ropes are stronger for a given thickness, more durable, and – a great advantage – remain soft and flexible when wet.

Rope control : (5) a sheet winch ; (6) a rigging screw (for tightening standing rigging) ; (7) a cleat ; and (8) a fairlead.

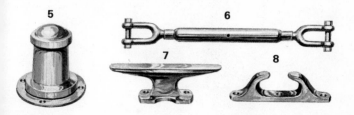

5

6

7

8

Steering gear

A sailing boat's steering gear consists of two main parts, a rudder and a tiller.

The **rudder** is a vertical board or plate which protrudes like a fin from the centre-line at the rear of the hull. It acts like a fin in that its inclination to one side or the other increases the resistance of the water on that side and causes the boat to swing in that direction.

Rudders are of various shapes, and some boats have lifting rudders, for convenience in shallow water. The rudders of many small boats, especially dinghies, can be easily shipped (slipped into place) and unshipped (removed).

The **tiller** is the horizontal bar by which the rudder is operated. It is in effect a lever which works about a fulcrum. Pushing the tiller to one side of the boat will incline the rudder in the opposite direction, and the boat's bows will therefore swing in the opposite direction to that in which the tiller has been moved.

Many dinghies may have extension pieces fitted to their tillers. This enables the helmsman to 'trim' (balance) the boat when necessary while sitting further forward than he would otherwise be able to do.

The tiller, which is almost always made of wood, is also usually an easily detachable unit which slides into or over the head of the rudder. It is a simple push-fit, with perhaps a pin to keep it in place.

Some larger boats have wheel steering, which reduces the effort demanded of the helmsman, but this type of gear is unnecessary in craft of the size described in this book.

A lifting rudder, shown in the normal (lowered) sailing position, and (dotted outline) in the raised position. This type of rudder is commonly found in dinghies.

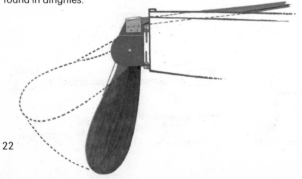

An old-fashioned rudder as formerly used on some ships' lifeboats, naval whalers and the like.

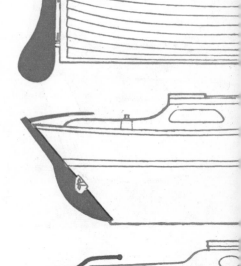

The streamlined rudder of a typical modern sailing-cruiser.

A separate, plate-type rudder on a fin-keeled boat.

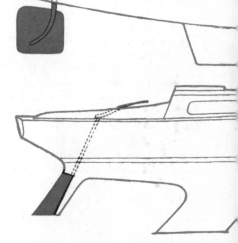

A modern type, faired into and attached to the skeg (the projection at the rear of the hull).

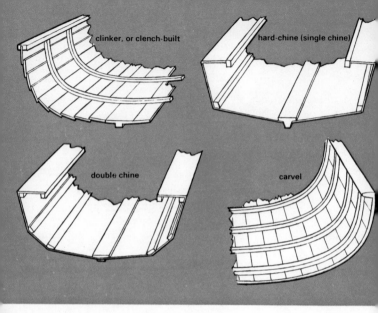

clinker, or clench-built

hard-chine (single chine)

double chine

carvel

Types of hull.

Hulls

Materials and methods of construction

Most sailing-boat hulls are made of wood or glass fibre. Some of the larger craft are built of steel.

Wooden hulls

The basic framework of the wooden hull should be constructed of something really tough, such as oak or elm. The wood most commonly used for the 'skin' – the hull covering – is mahogany. The skin may be planking or marine plywood.

The 'top' wood for boat construction is teak, but it is extremely expensive, and very heavy, and so is rarely used for smaller craft.

Hulls built with each of the planks overlapping the one below are said to be **clinker-built**. This is a traditional method of building which is still in wide use because it produces a strong, buoyant and comparatively cheap hull.

If the planks are fastened edge-to-edge to the framework of the boat, the hull is said to be **carvel-built**. This gives a smooth, rounded hull, but caulking is usually necessary between the planks as it is here that leaks may occur.

For **moulded** and **hard-chine** hulls, marine plywood is used. In the former type the plywood is moulded to the shape of the hull. In the latter, the hull is composed of broad, comparatively flat sheets of plywood, and there is a definite, sometimes sharp angle or chine between these sheets (usually between the sides of the hull and the bottom).

Glass fibre hulls

These are usually moulded all in one piece. There is a lot to be said for them in that they are very strong, do not leak, and are easy to maintain. On the debit side, they are sometimes rather unattractive to look at, and glass fibre is not a 'sympathetic' material to live with.

(*Below*) a glass fibre hull. The deck and cabin top are moulded as a separate unit and attached later. (*Bottom*) many National Twelves have clinker-built hulls; the Enterprise is a hard-chine boat.

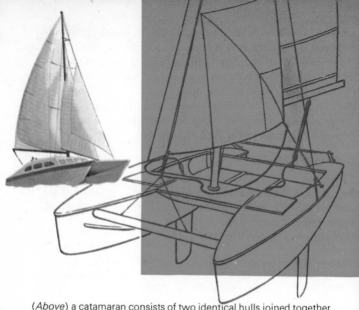

(*Above*) a catamaran consists of two identical hulls joined together by struts and a bridge-deck.

Multi-hulls

This is a convenient term to describe boats with more than one hull: catamarans (twin-hulled) and trimarans (triple-hulled).

Catamarans are twin-hulled craft whose design derives from that of native craft of the Pacific. They are notable for their speed, stability, and the smoothness with which they sail in rough water. A catamaran consists essentially of two identical hulls joined together by a flat deck, and is rigged in much the same way as the more conventional single-hulled craft. Also, as in the more conventional field, there are both racing (dinghy-style) and cruising catamarans.

Further advantages of the catamaran are its ability to sit upright when out of the water, and its comparatively shallow draught. A disadvantage is that a capsize may be more serious than it would be with a single-hulled boat. A capsized 'cat' tends to turn upside down. To prevent this, some 'cats' have a bulbous buoyancy chamber fitted to the top of the mast; ugly, but sensible.

Catamarans have proved themselves in both round-the-buoys racing, and in deep-water racing and cruising. A number of the larger ones have made notable ocean passages.

The **trimaran** has a main central hull with smaller float-hulls on either side. These craft have the same advantages as catamarans, plus an even greater stability factor, and they too have proved themselves in both racing and cruising. One disadvantage of the larger types is that their great beam may hamper them in a crowded anchorage.

Multi-hulls are still very much in the minority (yachtsmen are somewhat conservative people), but they are gaining favour all the time on both sides of the Atlantic.

Multi-hulls are normally rigged in the same way as single-hulled craft. As regards construction, it is essential that the lateral members should be strong enough to avoid a break-up in rough seas (this applies especially to the larger craft).

(*Below*) a cruising trimaran. Catamarans and trimarans carry the same rig as single-hulled craft.

Rigs

A boat's rig is determined by the number and positioning of her masts, and the number and shape of her working sails.

So far we have been discussing boats with the standard rig of today, that is, boats which have one mast and whose working or normal canvas consists of one sail in front of the mast and one behind it. However, a glance at the boats in most popular anchorages will show that some of them differ from this pattern. Some may have only one sail. Some may have two sails in front of the mast and one behind it. Some may have two masts, and proportionately more sails.

The boat we have been concerned with up to now – the boat with one mast and two sails – is a sloop, and is said to be **sloop-rigged**. Since this is by far the most popular rig nowadays, this book will be largely concerned with it.

(*Left*) a sloop, which has a working rig of a mainsail and one headsail ; (*right*) a modern cutter, with a working rig of mainsail and two headsails.

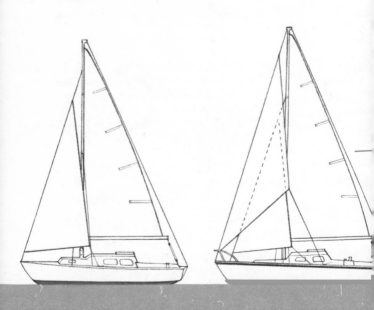

A lugsail dinghy.

Just a few very small boats have an even simpler rig than the sloop – just a single mast and one sail. In such cases the mast will be stepped (positioned) further forward than it is in a sloop.

One or two 'class' dinghies and certain others are rigged in this way, which is known as **lugsail rig**. In America it is known as **catboat rig**.

Because of its extreme simplicity, this kind of rig is particularly suited to single-handed sailing.

Cutter rig: a cutter is a boat which has a single mast, stepped a little further aft than that of a sloop, with two working sails in front of it and one behind it.

Cutter rig is good for tough sea-going work. It is not very suitable for very small boats, however, since in their case it is not practicable to break up the fore-canvas in this way (the individual sails would be too small). And even in boats of a fair size, the simplicity of sloop rig generally outweighs the particular advantages of cutter rig.

Catboat rig : this typically American rig consists of one large sail carried on a mast stepped well forward.

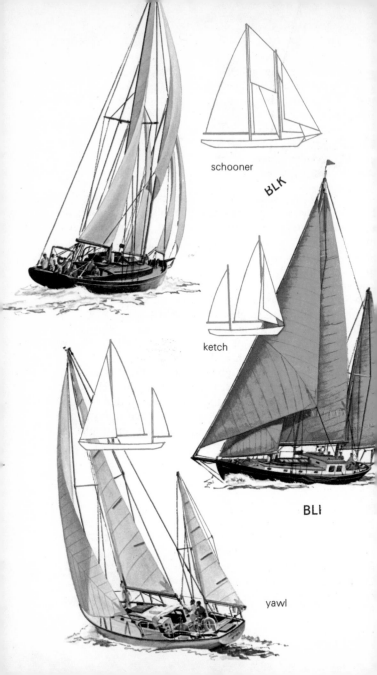

schooner

BLK

ketch

BLÍ

yawl

Two-masted rigs

The main reason for having more than one sail is to reduce the size of the largest unit of canvas to more manageable proportions (and the mast(s) to a reasonable height). For the same reason some boats have more than one mast, since this enables the total canvas to be split up still more, and the maximum mast-height to be reduced still further.

Generally speaking, two-masted rigs are found only in larger craft – those of at least seven or eight tons. Only comparatively large sailing vessels have more than two masts, and are quite outside the compass of this book.

There are three basic two-masted rigs:

Yawl rig is the most popular and efficient of the two-masted rigs. A yawl looks like a sloop or a cutter with a small extra mast near the stern. This is called the mizzen mast, and it carries the mizzen, or mizzen sail.

Quite a number of successful ocean racers are yawls, but this is not a rig for a very small boat. Below a certain size the mizzen is virtually useless; and in any case it is unnecessary to split up a small boat's canvas in such a way.

In **ketch rig** the mizzen mast is taller than that of a yawl, and stepped further forward. The mizzen sail is correspondingly larger and the mainsail proportionately reduced. This is a further step in reducing the size of the largest working sail, and ketches tend therefore to be larger than yawls.

Ketch rig is a cruising, not a racing rig, for the simple reason that it is not particularly efficient for sailing to windward (against the wind), which is all-important in racing.

In **schooner rig**, the masts are 'reversed'; the after one, which is further forward still than the mizzen mast of the ketch, is the taller. This is therefore the mainmast. The mast in front of it is the foremast.

Schooner rig is found only in craft of considerable size. It is even less efficient than ketch rig for windward sailing. For this reason there are very few schooner-rigged yachts, especially around Britain, because much of our sailing, and notably that which is done in narrow waters, has to be windward work. The rig is more common in American waters, and in particular on the eastern seaboard of the USA, where conditions suit it better.

Rig

Further identification by mainsail

A sailing craft's rig can be further identified by the kind of mainsail she has.

Most boats, as we have seen, have triangular mainsails. Such a sail is called **Bermudan** (**Marconi** in the USA), and the boat is said to be Bermudan (Marconi) rigged. A sloop with a triangular mainsail will therefore be a Bermudan (Marconi) rigged sloop, a cutter with such a sail will be a Bermudan (Marconi) rigged cutter, and so on.

Sometimes a boat will have a four-sided mainsail. There are two kinds of four-sided sail; one of them is virtually obsolete, the other is still in quite common use.

A four-sided sail has a spar at the top to support it. This spar is called the gaff.

In **gaff rig** the spar at the head of the sail sets at a considerable angle to the mast. This rig is seen nowadays chiefly on 'old-timers'. Its disappearance is again a matter of efficiency against the wind. A gaff mainsail is not so efficient to windward as a Bermudan sail, although it may be very effective with the wind abaft the beam. Another disadvantage of gaff rig is that it entails the use of an extra spar at the head of the sail and extra rigging to support it.

With **Gunter rig** the spar at the top of the sail is more nearly vertical. This rig comes closer to Bermudan rig, and its main merit is that it allows a boat to have a shorter mast. A number of popular small modern craft, including the little Mirror dinghy, are gunter-rigged.

The three most common types of mainsail. (*Left to right*) gaff, gunter and, the most efficient, Bermudan (Marconi).

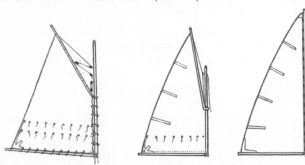

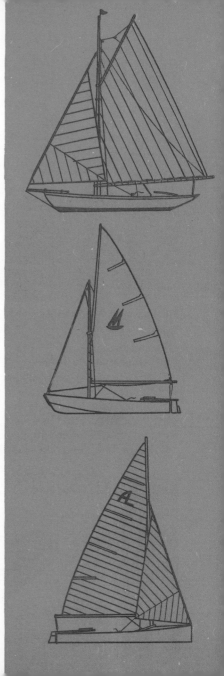

Modification of rig by mainsail, illustrated here on a sloop. Gaff rig is now mostly to be seen on older types of boat.

Gunter rig, once a familiar sight in British waters, has fallen almost completely out of favour except for small boats.

Although it uses a taller mast than other rigs, Bermudan (Marconi) rig is considered the most effective of all.

A trim sloop of about 7 tons, carrying mainsail and staysail.

Sails

What they are made of

Until comparatively recently all sails were made of canvas. A few still are, but, generally speaking, nylon, Terylene and other synthetic materials have now taken over.

Synthetic sails have many advantages. They are stronger; keep their shape better; can be stowed away damp, or even wet (canvas is subject to mildew). They exert more drive, last longer and need less maintenance. They are initially

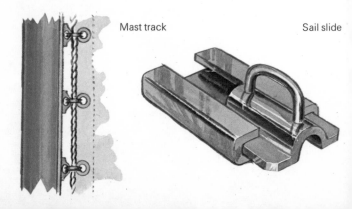

Mast track   Sail slide

more expensive than canvas sails, but their longer life compensates for this.

Attachment to spars

The tack of the jib is secured to a permanent fitting at the bows of the boat, and the luff is usually attached to the forestay by spring clips. The head is attached to the jib halliard.

Mainsails are attached to their spars in various ways – by slides, hoops, or lacing. The most common method of attaching the luff to the mast is by means of slides which work up and down a track on the mast.

The tack of the mainsail is secured to the forward end of the boom, and the head is similarly secured to the mainsail halliard. When the sail is fully hoisted, the luff should be taut between these two points.

The foot of the mainsail is stretched taut along the boom, usually by means of a light lashing attached to the cringle in the clew.

Additional Sails

As we have already seen, a boat may carry a balloon headsail (a spinnaker); or a staysail (Genoa), which is like a very large jib. Both these sails are 'extra-area' fair weather sails.

In heavy weather it may be necessary to reduce sail from the boat's basic or 'working' rig. This procedure is known as reefing, and may also involve the use of alternative sails.

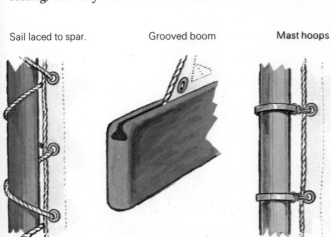

Sail laced to spar.   Grooved boom   Mast hoops

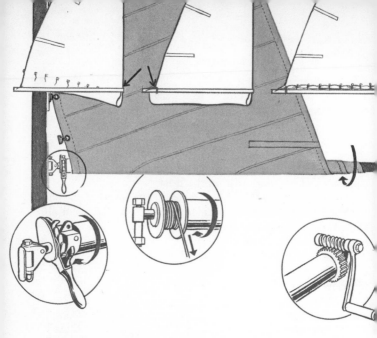

Reefing : with reef points : the sail is first made fast at the 'new' tack and clew, and the surplus foot is gathered up and the reef points tied around it. Almost all modern craft now have roller-reefing, three versions of which are illustrated here.

Reefing

In heavy weather it may be necessary to reduce sail from the boat's working rig to prevent her being overburdened.

Mainsail

In most old-fashioned craft, reefing was done by means of **reef points** – rows of short lengths of line attached to both sides of the mainsail, near the foot, and parallel to the boom. The area of the mainsail was reduced by lowering the sail the requisite amount, gathering up the foot of the sail, and tying the reef points round it (with reef-knots, of course). The forward and after ends of the 'new' foot were lashed to the boom through cringles provided for the purpose.

Reefing with reef points is a comparatively laborious

process, and most modern yachts have **roller-reefing** gear, which is much quicker and simpler to operate. For roller-reefing, the mainsail is lowered the requisite amount and the boom revolved by hand or by a mechanism at the forward end.

Foresails

If the area of the mainsail is considerably reduced, a reduction may have to be made in the area of the boat's fore-canvas. If she carries more than one foresail, this may be done by lowering one of them. In the case of a sloop, the area of the jib may be reduced by reefing, by either reef points or roller-reefing (in the latter case, the *luff* of the sail is rolled up by a special fitting); or, more commonly, by replacing the existing jib with a smaller one.

In very heavy weather a further reduction in area may be made by replacing the mainsail and fore-canvas with a storm trysail and storm jib, which are still smaller sails of heavier material more able to resist high wind.

A sloop with her mainsail reefed. The golden rule is : reef in good time. It is easier to shake out a reef than to put one in.

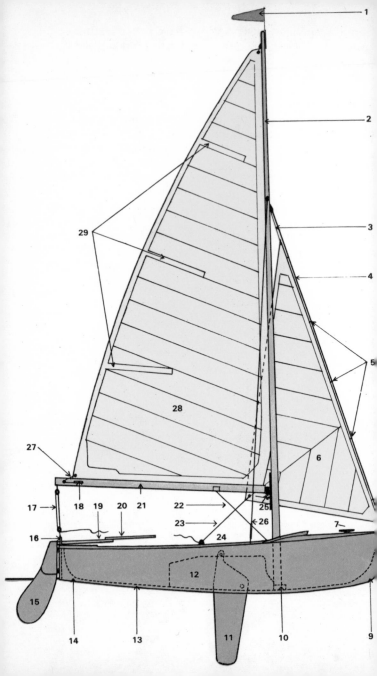

Parts of a sailing boat

The profile on the opposite page illustrates the main parts of one of the most popular of present-day sailing craft – the sloop-rigged dinghy. (For the sake of clarity the drawing is a simplified one.) You may like to compare this with another popular rig (shown on p. 32), the gunter rig, which is most commonly used on such small craft as the Mirror dinghy.

1 Burgee (or racing flag): indicates wind directions.
2 Mast: the main spar. Supports the sails.
3 Jib halliard: hoists jib.
4 Forestay: supports the mast (and jib) from forward.
5 Foresail hanks: attach luff of jib to forestay.
6 Jib: the single foresail characteristic of sloop rig.
7 Cleat: fitting for securing rope.
8 Bow plate: metal plate to which forestay is attached.
9 Stem: foremost part of hull.
10 Mast step: takes heel of mast.
11 Centreboard: retractable keel.
12 Centreboard case (or trunk): housing for centreboard.
13 Keel: fore-and-aft centre member.
14 Knee: strengthening member.
15 Rudder: alters direction of boat.
16 Mainsheet horse: metal traveller for mainsheet.
17 Mainsheet: controls angle of mainsail.
18 Outhaul cleat: for securing outhaul.
19 Tiller: lever for steering.
20 Tiller extension: increases length of tiller.
21 Boom: spar along which foot of mainsail is stretched.
22 Kicking strap: keeps the boom from lifting.
23 Jib sheet(s): control(s) angle of jib.
24 Fairlead: alters 'lead' of sheet.
25 Gooseneck: attaches mainsail boom to mast.
26 Shroud(s): lateral support(s) for mast.
27 Outhaul: stretches foot of mainsail.
28 Mainsail: the other sail-component of sloop rig.
29 Battens: support mainsail leech.

The design shown here is a characteristic example of the most efficient sailing craft so far developed. Its most important virtues are simplicity and ease of control. As regards rig, the same basic components are found on larger sloop-rigged craft, both on those with conventional single hulls, and on catamarans and trimarans. The keel arrangement is less typical, however; some cruising boats have centreboards, but these are not common nowadays, and most of the larger types of sailing craft have one or other of the various kinds of fixed keel.

AN ABC OF SAILING

When a boat is sailing with the wind blowing from astern, she is **running**. When the wind is coming from broadside-on, she is **reaching**. When it is blowing from ahead, she is **beating**.

These three directions of sailing merge into each other. A boat which is running may alter course (or the wind may change direction) until she has the wind more or less on the beam (broadside-on) when she will be reaching. If she alters course still further towards where the wind is coming from (or if the wind draws ahead) she will be beating.

The angle at which the sails are 'set' to the wind will be the same for both dinghies and larger craft on each of these directions of sailing.

Crew positions

In large craft, everyone will normally remain aft in the cockpit on all these directions (usually, but not necessarily, keeping to the windward side when reaching or beating). In the case of dinghies, the helmsman (and crew, if any) will keep up to windward when reaching or beating, and amidships to port and starboard when running (though this is less vital). This is because (see earlier) the people in a dinghy are an essential factor in its stability and 'balance'. When reaching or beating, their weight is needed on the windward side, to counteract the capsizing force of the wind, and when running they should sit amidships to keep the boat trimmed (i.e. level) fore and aft. In a bigger boat the weight of the crew is not an important factor.

In some dinghies one of the crew may sit on the end of a portable board projecting at right angles from the hull to increase the righting effect of his own weight when reaching or beating. In others, he may lean outboard, with his feet on the gunwale and his weight supported by a trapeze suspended from the masthead.

The direction in which a boat is sailing relative to the wind is known as its point of sailing. There are, therefore, three main points of sailing: (1) *with* the wind (running), (2) *across* the wind (reaching), (3) *against* the wind (beating).

The three points of sailing : when a boat has the wind astern, she is said to be running :

with the wind on the beam she is reaching ;

when she is heading into the wind she is beating.

The positions of a dinghy's helmsman and crew when the boat is running with jib goosewinged. In the diagram, the jib is blanketed by the mainsail.

Running

A boat is running when the wind is coming from astern. On this point of sailing the mainsail must be adjusted so that it is as nearly as possible at right-angles to the wind. The mainsheet, which controls the angle of the mainsail, must be slacked off until the sail is more or less at right-angles to the fore-and-aft line of the boat.

With the wind coming from astern, the jib will be blanketed by the mainsail, and the wind will not fill it. If the wind is coming from pretty well dead astern, the jib may be 'goosewinged' out on the other side of the boat (a pole of some kind will usually be needed to hold the clew of the sail out); and on this point of sailing the spinnaker may be hoisted.

When a boat is running the wind exerts no appreciable lateral thrust, so the keel, if it is a retractable one, may be raised to reduce the drag of the hull through the water.

Although it may appear so, running is not the easiest point of sailing. On the other points the wind exerts a steadying effect on the sails. This does not happen when the wind is coming from astern, and the boat is therefore more liable to roll. Steering may also be difficult when running, especially on the sea. The boat may yaw (swing) from side to side, especially if the keel has been raised. For this reason the keel may be kept partly lowered.

Gybing

When running, the wind should be kept at least fractionally on the opposite side of the boat from that on which the mainsail is set. If the wind is allowed to get round onto the 'wrong' side of the sail, it is likely to swing violently right across the boat – with nothing to stop it, since the mainsheet has been eased right out. This violent swing of the mainsail from one side to the other is known as a gybe, and in certain conditions can result in either a capsize or—even more serious—a dismasting.

Sailing on a very broad reach (with the wind on the quarter – coming from diagonally astern) and with the spinnaker set.

Reaching

A boat is reaching when the wind is coming from the beam (sideways-on). To catch the wind when reaching, the sails must be sheeted in closer than they are when the boat is running.

The wind-direction on which a boat may be said to be reaching varies over a wide arc. If the wind is coming from forward of the beam, the boat is said to be close-reaching, or on a close reach. This is because the wind is blowing from a point closer to the bow than to the stern. If the wind is coming from further aft, the boat is broad-reaching, or on a broad reach.

To catch the wind on a close reach, the sails must be sheeted in closer than they would be on a broad reach.

How close?

It will be obvious if the sails have not been sheeted in enough because the wind will not fill them properly. It is more difficult to tell whether they have been sheeted in too close. The best guide here is the luff of the mainsail (the part nearest the mast). The luff should be 'soft', that is, only gently pressed by the wind. Under those conditions, it will probably 'lift' occasionally.

When reaching, the wind will exert a capsizing force on the boat. This is why a boat on such a point of sailing heels over away from the wind. On a reach, the crews of dinghies place themselves to the best advantage on the windward side to counteract this force (see page 40).

If the wind is not too strong, a staysail (Genoa) may be hoisted in place of the jib. On a very broad reach, a spinnaker may be set.

Reaching is the fastest point of sailing. By the same token, it can also be the most exhilarating. It is also the easiest point for steering, and the safest direction in which to sail. There is no danger of gybing (as when running) and none of the problems which may be met with when beating.

The angle at which the sails are presented to the wind is more important when reaching than when running, and becomes still more important when beating, as we shall see in the next section.

WIND

Reaching. (*Above*) helms-man and crew sitting up to windward to counteract the heeling force of the wind. (*Right*) a small cruiser on a reach.

Beating requires more judgement than any other point of sailing.

Beating

No boat will sail *directly* against the wind. A boat is beating when the wind is coming from *diagonally* ahead, from a point fairly close to the bow. The sails must be sheeted in still closer than they are when reaching.

How close?

The same considerations apply as in the case of reaching. If the sails have not been sheeted in enough the wind will not fill them properly. If they have been sheeted in too much, they will be too 'hard'.

Beginner's error

One of the commonest mistakes made by beginners is to sheet the sails in too hard, and/or to try to sail too close to the wind (too directly towards the wind).

It is only too easy, when sailing thus, to bring the wind

too directly ahead, so that it exerts no thrust on the sails at all and they fail to fill properly. The boat will lose way (speed) and may stop, in which case it will be out of control, because the rudder has no effect on a boat which is not moving through the water. If the wind is boisterous, and variable in direction, a sudden gust may heel her right over, and even, if she is a dinghy, capsize her.

In suitable conditions, try sailing too close to the wind (that is, too much towards the direction the wind is coming from), with the sails sheeted in too hard. The boat's progress will be sluggish, and she will 'crab' sideways. Now 'start' the sheets – let them out a little – and head the boat a little further away from the wind. You will be surprised at how she at once surges forward.

Beating takes skill, because the estimation how close you can sail to the wind, and the correct angle of the sails, needs much more precision of judgement than on any other point of sailing.

A Vivacity class sloop beating to windward. Note that the sails are sheeted much closer in than they are on the other points of sailing.

(*Left*) the secret of good helmsmanship is to use as little rudder as possible. (*Right*) the use of a tiller extension. (*Opposite left*) wind direction indicators—burgee (racing flag) and tape. (*Opposite right*) weather helm.

Helmsmanship

The helmsman's most important job is to make sure that the boat is in motion at all times. This is known as

Steerage-way

If the boat has no steerage-way the rudder will be useless, and the boat not under control. This can be a dangerous state of affairs. She may suffer a 'knock-down' (be blown over) before she can get moving again ('under way').

Not too much rudder!

Any major alteration of her course should be made decisively; otherwise the helmsman should use the rudder as little as possible, since putting it over causes drag and reduces the boat's speed.

There is also a delay between the action of putting the helm over and the boat's response to it. The helmsman must therefore anticipate any alteration of course, and also ensure that the boat does not swing past the new course. If he fails to do this he will be doing too much steering, with the boat swinging first one way and then the other.

Wind indication
The helmsman needs some visual indication of wind direction. This is usually provided by a burgee, or racing flag, at the masthead, or by short lengths of string or tape tied to the shrouds.

Weather and lee helm
When sailing a straight course it should be necessary to hold the tiller a little over to the side of the boat the wind is coming from. This is a built-in safety device; if the tiller is let go (accidentally, or in an emergency) the boat will turn into the wind. This is not a desirable state of affairs, but it is better than 'lee helm'.

If the tiller has to be held towards the lee side of the boat (the side opposite that the wind is blowing from) she is said to carry lee helm. If the tiller is let go the boat may turn stern-on to the wind, and gybes and all sorts of other misfortunes may follow.

Mainsheet
In small craft, especially dinghies, the helmsman's other responsibility is the control of the mainsheet.

The mainsheet is the boat's other safety device. Letting it out will spill the wind from the mainsail and ease the boat.

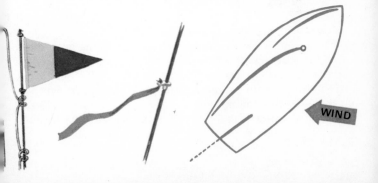

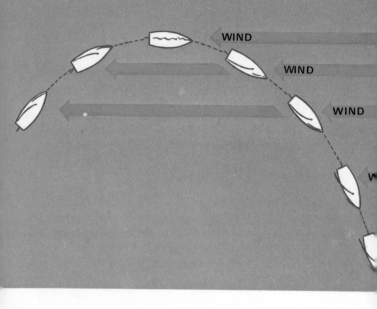

The successive stages in 'going about' from one tack to the other.

Tacking

It is impossible to sail directly against the wind. So how do we reach a point directly up to windward? We do it by beating first to one side and then the other. This is known as tacking.

We may have to take a number of tacks to reach our objective, or we may be able to get there in a single 'zig-zag'. The number and length of the tacks will depend upon the room available for manoeuvre—the more lateral space you have, the larger your tacks can be.

Port tack ... Starboard tack

If the wind is blowing from the port side of the boat, she is on the port tack. If it is blowing from the starboard side, she is on the starboard tack.

It is important to know which tack both your own boat and any other sailing craft in your vicinity is on, since this is a vital aspect of the 'rule of the road' at sea (see page 114).

Going about

Altering course from one tack to the other is known as going about.

It is essential when going about that the manoeuvre is announced clearly, and in good time, and that it is decisively carried out. The helmsman is in charge of the manoeuvre, and it is his job to issue the necessary orders. The normal form of the latter is the warning, 'Ready about', followed by the executive command 'Lee-oh!'

When going about, the helmsman puts the tiller over, to bring the boat round on to the other tack, and if necessary adjusts the trim of the mainsail after it has swung across to the other side of the boat. The crew slacks off the jib on the side it is sheeted in, hauls it in and secures it on the other side.

The helmsman's orders *must* be clearly understood. He must also alter course decisively, otherwise the boat may fail to swing across from one tack to the other.

Tacking round a racing mark : these Merlins are coming up to the mark on the port tack and altering course round it onto the starboard tack.

Gybing

A gybe occurs when a boat is running and the wind gets round on the 'wrong' side of the mainsail. A boat should never be allowed to gybe accidentally. On the other hand, the *intended* gybe is a useful technique. Intentional gybes are of two kinds, uncontrolled and controlled.

Uncontrolled gybe

In this case the wind is deliberately brought round, or permitted to get round, on the 'wrong' side, and the mainsail is allowed to swing freely across the boat. This can be an important manoeuvre when racing, because it enables a change of course to be made quickly.

An uncontrolled gybe should always be a deliberate move and, in any except the very lightest conditions, should be undertaken only by an experienced helmsman.

Controlled gybe

This is a much more elaborate procedure. The stages are as follows.
(1) With the wind obliquely astern, (2) alter course *towards* it. (3) As you sail closer to the wind the sails must be sheeted in, so as progressively to reduce the arc of swing of the mainsail when gybing. (4) When you judge that the swing will not be too violent for the prevailing conditions, head the boat away from the wind again, without adjusting the mainsheet. The wind is brought astern and then round onto the 'wrong' side of the mainsail, and the boat will gybe.

An accidental gybe. The wind shifts from the weather side to the lee side. If it gets round on the wrong side of the mainsail, the boom will swing violently across and the boat may capsize either way.

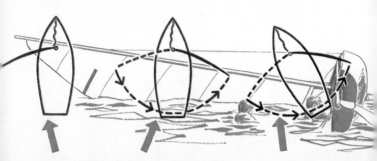

Wearing

When a boat is running in conditions which make gybing possible, it may be preferable to sail with the wind coming from directly astern. To maintain the boat's general direction down-wind, it may be necessary to alter course from time to time to bring the wind onto the other quarter. This procedure, which involves gybing, is really tacking down-wind, and is known as wearing.

Sometimes, if an alteration of course is needed while running, and the helmsman is not confident that he can gybe successfully, he may have to bring the boat round onto the wind until she is beating, then tack and pay right off (turn away from the wind) on that tack, so that he is turned in an almost complete circle.

Controlled gybe: the diagram shows the successive stages in this manoeuvre. The boat is brought round towards the wind and the mainsail is sheeted in. As the helmsman alters course away from the wind, the sail swings across through a limited arc. The mainsheet is then slacked away and the boat resumes her course.

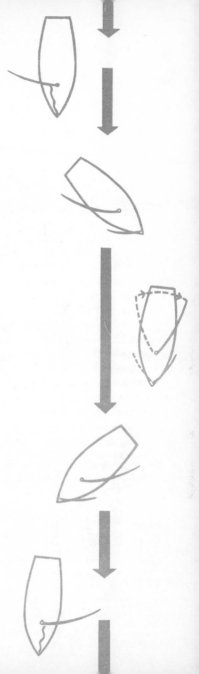

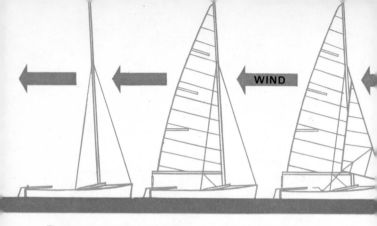

The stages in making sail. With the boat lying head to wind, the
mainsail is hoisted first, then the jib.

Making sail: getting under way

Sails should be hoisted only in circumstances in which they
will not catch the wind.

The mainsail is all-important. It should be hoisted only
when the wind is coming from ahead of the boat or, at most,
from the beam (in which case the mainsheet will have to be
slacked right off first so that the sail does not catch the wind).

Dinghies on shore can usually be manoeuvred into a
position in which at least the mainsail can be hoisted. If sail
is being made at anchor or on a mooring, the procedure may
be more complicated.

Getting under way: if the boat is lying head to wind, make sail, let go,
give the bows a sheer (perhaps by backing the jib). This will bring her
on to a beat. If the boat is lying stern to wind, hoist the jib, let go, turn
towards the wind, hoist the mainsail, proceed on a beat as before.

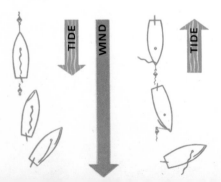

In still water there will be no problem, since the boat will lie with her bows facing the wind. The procedure in this case is to hoist the mainsail and then the jib.

If the tide or current is in the same direction as the wind, the boat will still be lying head to wind.

If the wind is blowing across the tide or current, the boat will probably be lying with the wind coming obliquely from ahead. The sails can be hoisted as above, so long as the sheets are slacked off to prevent the sails catching the wind.

If the wind is blowing against a strong tide or current, the boat may be lying more or less stern-on to the wind. In this case the jib is hoisted and the boat gets under way under that sail alone.

The angle at which a boat lies to the wind will depend upon what sort of boat she is, and the relative strengths of the wind and the tide or current. The procedure for getting under way is as follows:

Head to wind. Hoist the mainsail, then the jib. Weigh the anchor or cast off the mooring, sheering the bows away from the wind. Sheet in until the sails fill. The boat is then under way.

Beam wind. Make sail as above. Weigh the anchor or cast off the mooring. Sheet in until the sails fill.

Stern wind. Hoist the jib. Weigh the anchor or cast off the mooring. Sheet in the jib and sail down-wind until you have room to manoeuvre, then head to wind and hoist the mainsail.

How will the boat at (1) get away ? The answer (or one of them) : let go the mooring and drop back ; back the jib and trim the sheets on the port tack (2) ; come about on to the starboard tack (3) ; tack again at (4) and sail clear (5).

Trial trip

Let us now, by way of recapitulation, take a short 'round trip' out from the beach, jetty, mooring or anchorage and back again.

Let us suppose that the wind is blowing from the direction in which we want to start off, and that the boat is lying head to wind.

Hoist the mainsail, then the jib. Cast off, or weigh the anchor, sheering the bows away from the wind. Sheet in the sails until they fill. The boat is under way. Since she is sailing against the wind, she is *beating*.

To get any distance to windward, we shall probably have to *tack*, perhaps more than once.

Let us assume we have enough room to sail a triangular course. When we are sufficiently far up to windward, the bows can be headed away from the wind and the sheets eased until the wind is on the beam and the boat is *reaching*.

The next manoeuvre will be to alter course again in order to return to our starting point. To begin the return trip the helmsman will alter course still further away from the wind until it is *almost* astern. At the same time the sheets will be eased still further until the mainsail boom is almost at right-angles to the fore-and-aft line of the boat. The boat is now *running*.

Since steering is most difficult when sailing down-wind, the helmsman must be careful not to let the wind move round onto the 'wrong' side of the mainsail, or an accidental gybe may result. On the other hand the final alteration of course will probably require a deliberate gybe, or the more complicated manoeuvre of heading up into the wind and then paying off on the other tack.

The procedure for running ashore, coming alongside a jetty or the like, or anchoring or picking up a mooring, will depend on wind and tide/current conditions. Before we consider the necessary manoeuvres we will look at the way these forces affect a boat when she is sailing a course.

A recap of the points of sailing : the diagram opposite shows all three (start at any point, and follow them round). (*Below*) (1) running 'goosewinged', (2) sailing on a very broad reach — almost running. (3) beating (on the port tack).

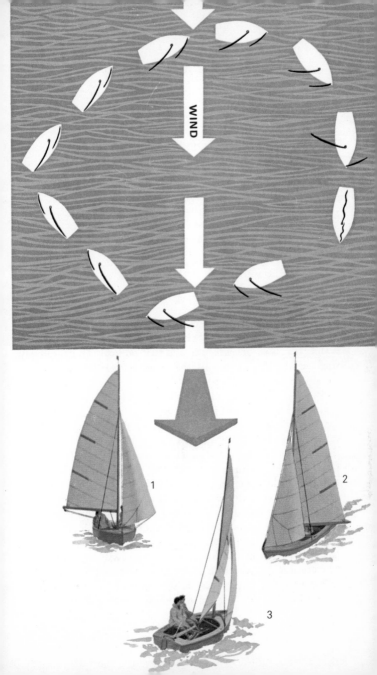

WIND

1

2

3

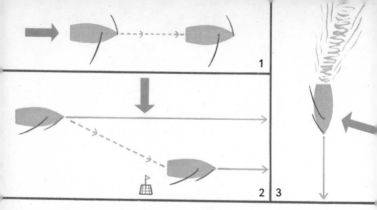

Leeway : when the wind is astern (1) it exerts no sideways thrust, so there is no leeway. When it is blowing across the boat's course, (2) it exerts thrust and leeway results. In diagrams (1) and (2) the actual course of the boat is indicated by the dotted line. In (3) the amount of leeway can be estimated from the angle between a boat's apparent direction and her wake.

Leeway

We have seen earlier that one function of a boat's keel is to provide resistance to her being blown sideways through the water. It is now necessary to add that no keel can completely prevent this happening. If the wind is exerting an oblique thrust on the boat there will always be an element of sideways 'slip'. This movement will obviously be away from the wind, to leeward, and is called leeway.

Other forces besides that of the wind may act on a boat under way. In a river she may be subject to the effects of the current, and, similarly, at sea she may be affected by tides or tidal streams. Depending on the boat's course relative to these movements of the water, her sideways drift will be increased, decreased, or cancelled out. If, for instance, she is sailing with a cross-current or tide moving in more or less the same direction as the wind, then obviously her leeway will be increased. Conversely, if the current or tide is moving against the wind, her leeway will be diminished. The amount by which her leeway is increased or diminished will depend upon the relative strengths of these movements of wind and water. If a strong tide is running against a light breeze, she may even have 'negative' leeway, that is, she may have a sideways drift to windward instead of to leeward.

Weathering a mark

When reaching or beating in still water, that is, when the wind is exerting a sideways thrust on your boat, you cannot reach a mark by sailing directly towards it. You must aim for a point to windward of the mark, to allow for the effects of leeway. In moving water you must also allow for the plus or minus factor of the tide or current.

You can judge your boat's leeway by looking astern at her wake and noting the angle it makes with her heading, although after a while you will rely on your judgement and experience to know what allowance to make to weather a given mark. Good judgement of this kind is of course an important factor in round-the-buoys racing.

A knowledge of tides and tidal streams is obviously important in estimating the effect of leeway on a passage. To estimate your progress 'over the ground' (that is, the distance and the course actually 'made good'), you will need to allow fairly precisely for the strength of the local tide and/ or tidal streams at a given time.

When rounding a mark (or to reach a desired position) allowance must be made for leeway.

Coming alongside, picking up a mooring, etc.

Never try to bring a boat to rest *with the wind astern and the mainsail up*—she will try to continue sailing, and in anything of a breeze, confusion and damage may result.

Head to wind

When circumstances permit, you should approach your finishing point head to wind. You should do this in such a way that, when you are a short distance from your objective, you can turn your boat directly into the wind and let her 'fetch' the remaining distance under her own momentum. When you have reached your objective, let go of the tiller and slacken off the sheets. If the boat is afloat, she will lie head to wind with her sails fluttering. She will not attempt to sail on, and the sails will be easier to lower.

In certain circumstances it may be necessary to run past your objective, then turn and beat back to it.

Picking up a mooring, etc. Basic manoeuvre: if a boat is approaching a mooring in the same direction as the wind (and tide or current), she will normally sail past and tack back up (2).

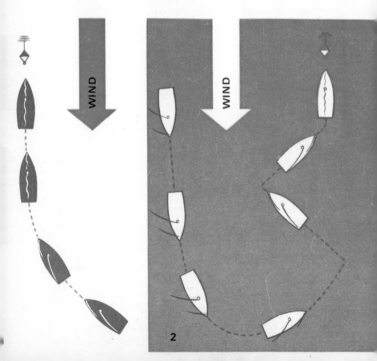

Wind astern

If you are approaching your objective with the wind astern and it is not possible to run past and beat back, you should turn head to wind while still some distance off, lower the mainsail, then turn again and run the remaining distance under jib alone. The jib should be lowered or slacked off as you come up to your objective.

Tide or current

If the tide or current is moving in the same direction as the wind, you can consider them as virtually one entity. If the tide or current is moving against the wind, think of *the way your boat will lie when she has come to rest.*

If the tide or current is so strong, relative to the wind, that when she stops sailing she is lying stern-on to the wind, you should approach the mooring or anchoring place under jib alone.

A boat approaching a mooring with the wind, but against the tide or current, should turn into the wind some distance off, lower her mainsail, then turn again and run up under jib alone (3). (*Right*) this manoeuvre performed in an anchorage.

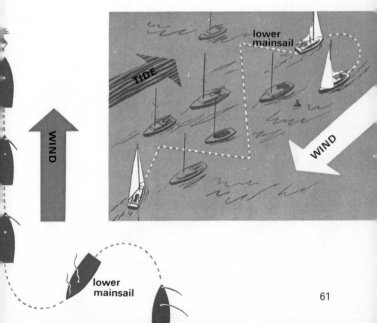

Lowering sails

As a general rule sails should be lowered only when a boat is lying head to wind, or at least when the wind is not blowing from astern. A boat's sails are stretched taut along their forward edge, and will blow out from that edge like a flag from a flagpole. If the boat is lying head to wind they will remain inboard and will be that much easier to deal with. With a beam wind, they will blow out on the opposite side and will be difficult to gather in. With a wind from astern, foresails will blow out over the bow and will be even harder to handle. As for the mainsail, this may cause real trouble. Since it is stretched taut along the boom as well as along the mast, it will not be free to blow out with the wind. A wind from astern will fill it, the boat will start sailing when you do not want it to, and the pressure of the wind on the sail will make it difficult to lower (see page 60). If the wind is strong, it may be impossible to lower the mainsail at all.

Rules for lowering sails

(1) If possible, lower your sails only when your boat is lying head to wind, or very nearly so (the tide may have an effect on her 'lie').

(2) Lower the foremost sail first, then work progressively aft, lowering the aftermost sail last. In a sloop, this will mean lowering the jib first, then the mainsail. If you lower your after sails first, the bows may blow away from the wind.

The mainsail of a cruiser is normally left on between trips. A sail cover protects it from wind and rain.

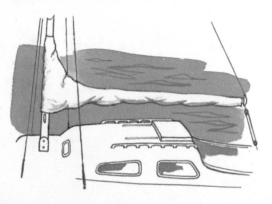

Stowage of sails

Sails should never be lowered and left unsecured. The mainsail, if it is not removed completely, should be tied at intervals to the boom, preferably with sail-ties (these are narrow strips of canvas or, more frequently nowadays, Terylene or the like). Foresails, if not removed straight away, should be tied to some part of the boat, such as a guardrail.

Sail storage below (this applies to cruisers) should preferably be in sail bags. This protects them and makes for the tidiness which is so important in a restricted space. The bags should be marked ('working jib', 'staysail', 'spinnaker' etc.) so you know just where to find the sail you want.

A dinghy's sails are usually removed completely after use and taken ashore. A cruiser's mainsail may be left on the boom, preferably protected by a sail cover. Nowadays sail covers, like the sails themselves, are usually made of Terylene or some other synthetic fibre, and less frequently of canvas.

The diagram shows the stages in lowering the sails of a boat lying head to wind – the jib first, then the mainsail.

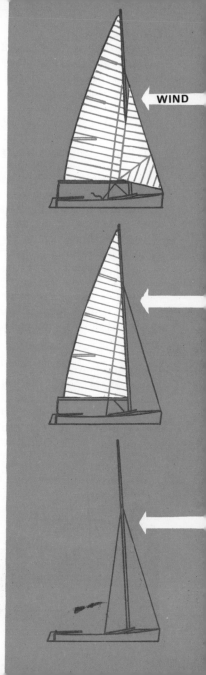

WIND

Dinghies for fun

Someone once said 'the smaller the boat, the greater the fun', and this has a good deal of truth in it. On the other hand it is not true to say that the smaller the boat, the easier she will be to sail. A cruising boat of, say, four or five tons, will be much more tolerant of any mistakes you may make, whereas with a dinghy, responsive to every puff of wind and every touch of the tiller, there is little room for errors.

Sailing dinghies range in length from eight to twenty feet. Their hulls are of wood, glass fibre or, occasionally, metal. All carry a working rig of one or two sails. They all have retractable keels. Some of them are half-decked, that is, decked in as far aft as the mast. Some of them have 'sawn-off' bows (like the pram dinghy tenders mentioned later). Because of the danger of swamping or capsizing, some of them have buoyancy compartments which are either built-in or, more commonly, in the form of buoyancy bags.

Because of the danger of capsizing, all dinghy sailors should wear life jackets at all times.

Some sailing dinghies are simply 'mongrels', but the majority belong to recognized classes, which will be dealt with later.

Camping dinghies

A dinghy of reasonable size may be used for camping-cruising. Such a boat should preferably be half-decked, to provide dry stowage for gear. At night a tent is made by rigging a tarpaulin, or its equivalent, over the boom.

A camping dinghy in a quiet anchorage.

Some popular 'knockabout' dinghies. (*Top to bottom*) Optimist; Wayfarer; Mayfly; Top Ten; Duckling; Gull.

Racing Dinghies 1

You can, of course, race in any kind of dinghy provided that you can find someone to race against. If, however, your boat does not belong to any recognized class, you may find this difficult. Mixed craft can only compete satisfactorily on a handicap basis, and this is hard to organize and is rarely done among dinghy sailors.

Excluding handicap racing, there are three racing classes. The basic principle governing these classes is that all the boats in a given class shall be alike in certain fundamental respects, and therefore in their potential performance. These classes are:

Formula Class

The boats in such a class are basically all alike but may vary a little in the shape of the hull, sail area, and equipment. The essential here is that these various factors, when expressed mathematically, should add up to the same result.

Restricted Class

As in the case of formula class boats, those in a restricted class can vary a little in hull design and sail area, but they are not controlled by an overall formula. This means that you cannot compensate for a saving on the hull requirement by increasing the sail area beyond a specified limit.

One-Design Class

Boats in these classes are more alike than those in the classes previously noted, in that only very minor variations are permitted.

The second and third of the above classes are also often subject to other regulations, such as how often you can have new sails, or how many times you may scrub off the boat's bottom or repaint the hull. The object here is to prevent people with more time and money than others from obtaining an advantage.

Some racing dinghies : (*Above, left to right*) Firefly ; International 14 ; National 12 ; (*Below, left to right*) Flying Dutchman (International) ; Merlin Rocket ; Snipe (International).

Racing dinghies 2

Now let us look at some of the most popular of present day dinghies, starting with the cheerfully named Optimist. Only 7′ 6″ long, this One-Design cockleshell is of American design. Originating in Florida, it became very popular in Europe, and is now gaining favour in Britain.

The Optimist is essentially a children's boat, but the children's boat *par excellence* is the International Cadet ('International' means it is a recognized international class). The Cadet is 10′ 6″ long and has a pram bow. Many young people have learned the ropes in Cadets, graduating to other boats later.

Somewhat further up the size-scale, we come to twelve-foot boats such as the National Firefly (National means it is a recognized class in Britain), and the popular National 12, which is a Restricted Class Boat. Then, at thirteen feet, there is the National Enterprise. At 13′ 6″ there is the International Snipe which originated, like the Optimist, in Florida, and is the largest class in the world.

More racing dinghies (*On this page, left to right*) Hornet; Finn (International); Lightning (International); Cadet (International). (*On the opposite page*) 505 (International) Graduate; Enterprise; GP 14.

Then there are various boats around the fourteen-foot
mark: the GP (General Purpose) 14, which was designed to be
equally suitable for either family sailing or racing; the
National Merlin Rocket, which is a larger and faster sister of
the National 12; the International Finn (14′ 9″) which is unusual in that it has a single sail, a flexible mast, and no stays
(shrouds); and the International 14, one of the aristocrats of
the dinghy-racing world.

Among the largest boats of all are the National Hornet (16′)
in which the crew sits out on a sliding seat to increase the
'righting factor'; the International 505 (16′ 6″), and the huge
International Flying Dutchman (19′ 10″) in both of which the
crew sits out on a trapeze.

These are just a few of the many kinds of dinghy in
existence today. Most of them can of course be used for
pottering about as well as racing.

N.B. All the boats described here are illustrated on pages 64–9.

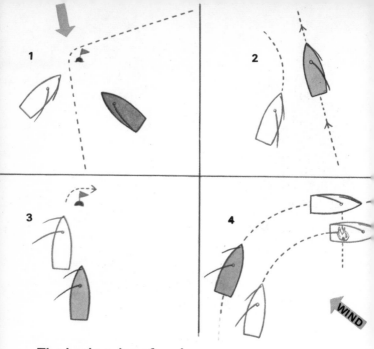

The basic rules of racing

The rules of yacht racing have developed from the basic Rules of The Road At Sea, and are administered by the International Yacht Racing Union. The situations in which these basic rules apply, illustrated in Figures 1–4 above, are as follows:

(1) A yacht on the port tack or gybe shall keep clear of a yacht on the starboard tack or gybe. The only exception to this rule is when there is an obstruction which impedes the port-tack yacht from taking avoiding action.

(2) A windward yacht shall keep clear of a leeward yacht. The situation in which this rule most commonly applies is shown in Figure 2, where the blue boat is tacking to the windward mark and the white boat is reaching away from it.

(3) A yacht establishing an overlap on another at a mark shall have right of way at that mark. In Figure 3, therefore, the blue boat has the right of way.

(4) All yachts racing shall make every effort to avoid a collision.

It is advisable to obtain a copy of the current racing rules from the Royal Yachting Association as soon as you begin to race seriously, or you may find yourself giving way in situations which could be turned to advantage by a thorough knowledge of the rules.

The start

Starting tactics vary greatly with the type of race you are sailing; a club race on a lake will require totally different tactics from a championship race at sea.

There are three basic points to remember, all of which will be obvious after your first start. Firstly, you should be on the line as the gun goes. (An important point here is that you should always look for the gunsmoke rather than listen for the noise.) Secondly, your boat should be travelling at maximum speed when the gun goes (see the illustrations below). Thirdly, it is vital that you be far enough from other boats for your wind to be unimpeded (some of those below are poorly placed).

The start

At the windward mark

(1) the right-hand boat has the advantage of a free wind while blanketing the other.
(2) the upper boat has the advantage of being on the starboard tack. The other must give way.
(3) at the leeward mark, try to establish an overlap.
(4) aim at the most favourable part of the finishing line.

Mid-race tactics/the finish

After the start the boats will spread out in an attempt to find a clear wind as they tack to the windward mark. In most dinghy races it is difficult to know your position until the first mark is reached, and it is important to observe on this first leg what other boats are doing, and perhaps above

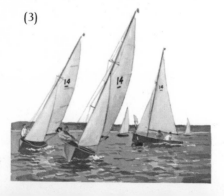

all what the wind and tide or current conditions are like.

The two main points to remember on the first leg or beat are, firstly, not to overstand the mark – that is, not to sail further than is necessary; and secondly, to approach the mark on the starboard tack. This will give you the right of way over boats approaching on the port tack (see pages 120–1).

At the first mark you will decide whether to sail an attacking or a defensive race. Obviously if you are leading you will sail defensively, but if you are half-way down the fleet the choice may be more difficult, since by attacking boats in front you may leave yourself open to those behind.

Tactics on down-wind legs of the course may be summed up as blanketing your opponents while keeping your own wind clear. On a run you sit right behind your opponent and cut off his wind altogether. As you pass him, he will probably luff you, and the situation shown in Figure (4) will develop. In this it is vital that the centreboard or dagger board be lowered, or you will slide sideways into him and be disqualified. Generally speaking, the wider you and your opponent are spread, the better.

At the leeward mark, you should try to get an overlap so as to slip through your opponent. To windward, always attempt to keep between your opponent and the mark, if defending; and if attacking him, stop your opponent 'covering' you, that is, cutting off your wind supply, as in Figure (1). Tactics at the finish are exactly the same, except that you should watch the angle of the finishing line and try to cross it at the most favourable point.

(4)

Cruising

Sailing may be broadly divided into two main kinds – racing and cruising. Racing involves sailing a prescribed course, in competition with other boats. Cruising is non-competitive, and may be described as 'touring by water'. Cruising boats usually sail alone, free to choose their own course.

Cruising normally involves remaining aboard for a considerable period of time, so certain fundamentals of accommodation are necessary. These are: a cabin (as protection from the weather); bunks; some means of cooking (usually a paraffin or bottled-gas stove); and some form of sanitation (a five-tonner may have a flush toilet, a two-and-a-half-tonner may have to make do with a bucket).

Cruising can be subdivided again into three kinds: cruising in inland waters; in estuaries and sheltered coastal waters; and on the open sea. Britain, as we have seen earlier, has few inland waterways suitable for cruising under sail and such areas as exist are largely given over to hire craft, so this form of the sport has comparatively few devotees among private owners. The majority of small cruisers are to be found sailing in sheltered waters such as the Solent, and along heavily indented coasts such as those of Essex and Suffolk. Cruising on the open sea is an altogether more rugged business, and is not to be recommended for the beginner.

Remember that although the smallest (well-built) boat will be capable of going almost anywhere, her crew may not be. It is important therefore that the beginner does not try to do anything beyond his capabilities.

It is important, too, that a boat should be not only properly designed and soundly built, but also *well-found*. This means that her gear – rigging, sails, steering equipment, ground tackle (anchor and cable) and so on – must be maintained in sound condition. If she has an auxiliary engine, it should be reliable. An engine that fails to work when it is needed is worse than none at all, since you may instinctively come to depend upon it in certain situations.

It is always a good idea to plan the details of your cruise on paper before you set out. If you do this, you will have a note of what courses to steer and what hazards to avoid.

(*Above*) the five-ton Vertue class sloop is a rugged little sea-going cruiser. (*Below*) cruising on inland waters brings its own particular satisfactions. Boats of this kind frequently have masts which can be lowered (for passing under bridges), and in many the cabin top can be raised, to allow more room when not under way.

(*Above*) profile of a typical small cruising sloop with a fixed keel.
(*Below*) a boat of this kind under way (beating on the starboard tack).

Cruisers

The smallest practical boat for cruising in any degree of comfort is the two-and-a-half-tonner, which will be about 18 feet long. If she is an oldish boat, she may have a centreboard. An increasing number of small modern cruisers have bilge keels, and most of them are sloop-rigged.

Almost all cruising boats now have some form of auxiliary

power. In the case of the smallest, this is usually an outboard motor.

We have said before, but it will bear repeating, that a cruising boat must be well-found (that is, sound) in her hull, spars, rigging, sails, auxiliary power, etc. If you start off with a new boat you should have no worries in this respect, at least to begin with, but careful annual maintenance will be necessary. *Any important damage or weakness should be dealt with before going to sea again.*

You must be very careful when buying a second-hand boat. *Do not go by appearances.* A boat that has been laid up for some time may look dilapidated, but be in fact quite sound. Conversely, a coat of paint can hide serious defects.

It is always advisable to have a second-hand boat, especially a wooden boat, inspected by a competent marine surveyor, or at least by some knowledgeable and impartial person. Remember, *your life may depend upon it.*

The 'accommodation' of a small cruising boat is determined not only by the amount of space below decks, but also by the capacity of the **cockpit**. The average two-and-a-half-tonner will comfortably accommodate two people, both in the cockpit and below decks; a four- or five-tonner will hold four.

Some cockpits are self-draining. In other words, they are fitted with drainpipes which will empty the cockpit if a sea fills it. This is, however, a deep-sea precaution, and the smallest boats are not all so equipped.

Ground tackle: every small cruiser should carry an adequate anchor and an anchor chain (or rope) of suitable length and calibre.

Cockpit of the same small cruising boat, showing tiller, sheet winches, mainsheet and divided backstay.

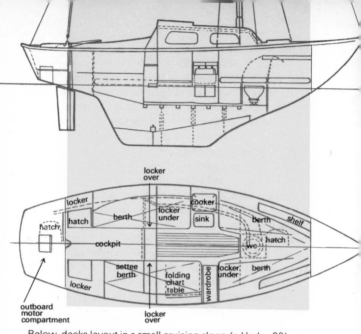

Below-decks layout in a small cruising sloop (a Harley 22).

Below decks

The space below decks on a small cruiser may be divided into accommodation, stowage and living facilities.

Accommodation. The average two-and-a-half-tonner will have two berths, and the four- or five-tonner will have three or four. Remember that the older the boat is, the less accommodation she is likely to have.

Normally there will be two berths in the cabin amidships, and in a two-and-a half tonner this is likely to be the total accommodation. A larger boat may have one, or perhaps two additional berths in the forepeak (the part forward of the cabin). These forward berths may be permanent ones, or they may be 'pipe-cots'. A pipe-cot is, essentially, a piece of canvas stretched over a frame of piping. When not in use, it can be stowed against the boat's side, to save space.

An important aspect of a boat's accommodation is her headroom. Full or standing headroom means that anyone not abnormally tall can stand up anywhere in the cabin; this is not as a rule to be found in boats of less than five tons. In most boats the after end of the cabin is raised (this is called a 'doghouse') and in the larger of the boats we are discussing it should be possible to stand up here, if not elsewhere. Even the smallest boats have 'sitting headroom' which means it is possible to sit up straight on the berths in the cabin.

Stowage. There will normally be stowage space for sails and other gear in the forepeak, and perhaps under the cockpit seats. Personal gear is stowed in lockers in the cabin and there are sometimes special stowages for cooking utensils and so on. Some of the larger boats in our range may have special hanging lockers for oilskins and the like.

Living facilities. There will normally be some form of cooking stove (usually bottled gas or paraffin), and there must be some sanitary provision, however crude. As indicated earlier, a bucket may have to do. Where space permits, a boat may have a flush toilet. This will be in the forepeak, forward of the cabin. The old adage 'a place for everything and everything in its place' has more meaning on board a small boat than almost anywhere else. Not being able to find what you need may at best be annoying; at times, it can be positively dangerous.

View of the interior of a small cruising boat, looking aft.

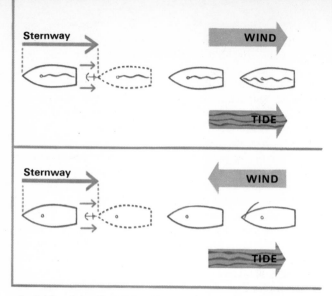

Anchoring : bring the boat up head to tide or current (the procedure is the same as for coming up to a mooring), lower the anchor and drop back. Remember that you must judge where the boat will lie after she has come to rest.

Anchors and cables

Two types of small-boat anchor are in general use today. These are the 'fisherman's' anchor and the CQR.

The fisherman's anchor is the traditional one. It consists of a shank, at the bottom of which is a curved crosspiece ending in two prongs, called flukes, and at the top, a bar, at right-angles to the crosspiece, which acts as a trip-bar and

Types of anchor (1) fisherman's (2) CQR (the most popular nowadays) (3) mushroom.

causes one of the flukes to dig in. When the anchor is not in use the trip-bar lies along the shank for ease of stowage.

The CQR anchor is a more modern design and is almost standard on new boats nowadays. It is shaped like a plough-share, and has much greater holding power than a fisherman's anchor of the same weight (which means that a lighter anchor can be used). It is easy to stow, and the anchor cable is less likely to foul it because it has no exposed fluke.

The **cable** should be strong enough, and long enough, to hold your boat in any circumstances she may normally encounter. One of the principles of anchoring is that you should veer (let out) cable equal to three times the depth of water in which you are anchoring. This is because the drag of the cable along the sea or river bed is an important element in the holding power of your ground tackle. You will there-fore need a cable at least three times as long as the maximum depth in which you are likely to drop anchor.

Anchoring

Judge where you want your boat to lie *when you have let out your cable*. Then bring her up ahead of that point, head to tide or current, or head to wind in still water. Wait until the boat begins to drop back, then lower away, controlling the cable all the time.

Remember that you must anchor in a place where there is room for your boat to swing to a change of tide or wind, and that in tidal waters you must allow for (1) the maximum depth of water at high tide, and (2) sufficient depth of water at low tide, unless you are prepared to go aground.

At anchor: sufficient cable should be veered for part of it to lie along the bottom. Golden rule: veer roughly three times the depth of water (in tidal waters, three times the maximum depth).

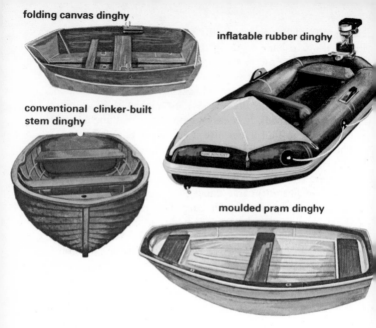

folding canvas dinghy

inflatable rubber dinghy

conventional clinker-built
stem dinghy

moulded pram dinghy

Dinghy tenders

However small your cruising boat, you will probably need a
dinghy for getting to and from her home mooring, and/or for
going ashore and back again when she is anchored or moored
elsewhere.

These little dinghies are of various kinds: wooden, built
either clinker style or of marine plywood; glass fibre; of
collapsible wood-and-canvas construction, and inflatable
rubber. The latter two kinds have the advantage of being
more easily stowed aboard, and the last kind has the addi-

The dinghy may be towed astern or carried aboard (on the foredeck or
cabin top). Carrying it aboard is preferable, since the dinghy will not
then be a hazard in rough weather, nor affect the parent boat's speed.

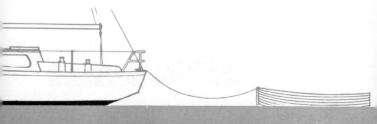

tional merit that in an emergency it will serve as a quite efficient lifeboat. Of the rigid dinghies among the foregoing, many will have 'sawn-off' (pram) bows, to reduce their length and facilitate stowage.

Stowage
A collapsible wood-and-canvas dinghy or an inflatable one can be carried aboard on even the smallest cruiser, although it may be necessary to carry it on deck.

It will not be possible to carry a rigid dinghy aboard anything smaller than a four- or five-tonner. When such a boat is carried aboard, it may occupy one of two positions: (1) on the cabin-top, if the height of the boom above the cabin-top gives sufficient clearance; or (2) on the foredeck (possibly over the forehatch, if there is one). Whichever of these two positions the dinghy occupies, it should be firmly secured, preferably with gripes specially made for the purpose.

Towing
Many small cruisers find it necessary to tow their tenders, but there are advantages in carrying these little boats aboard. Towing a dinghy will appreciably reduce the parent boat's speed, and it will be one more thing to keep an eye on. Also, a dinghy at the end of a tow rope can be a nuisance when the parent boat is at anchor, bumping and scraping the larger boat under certain conditions of wind and tide or current.

Safety
You can propel these little boats by either oars or a small outboard motor – it is up to you. It is also up to you not to overload them. More accidents happen between the parent boat and the shore than almost in any other circumstances.

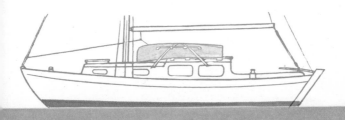

More about cabin boats

A number of popular British and American cabin boats are illustrated on this and the following three pages. Some of them are rather larger than those we have discussed so far, but it is perhaps no bad thing to look ahead for a moment. It is a widespread weakness among small-boat sailors – cruising men anyway – that no sooner have they acquired a small boat and sailed her for a while than they start yearning after something bigger.

The term 'cabin boat' is used here because, although the general emphasis may be on cruising, a large number of cabin boats are in fact 'class' boats too, and spend a good deal or even all of their time racing. The very popular and successful South Coast One Design (SCOD) illustrated on page 87 is a notable example of such a boat.

What to Buy

When you come to the point of buying a cabin boat, two main points will have to be taken into consideration. These are (1) how many people do you anticipate will be regularly sailing aboard her, and (2) how much can you afford to spend? These two aspects may well decide whether you buy a new boat or a second-hand one; if you want to take your family sailing, for instance, and your pocket is limited, you may have to settle for a second-hand boat rather than a new one because, generally speaking, you will be able to buy a bigger second-hand boat for your money.

It is most important that, whichever boat you buy, her accommodation should be adequate for the number of people who will regularly be sailing in her. It is all very well to say that it doesn't matter that you only have three berths instead of the four you really need because junior can sleep on the cabin sole (floor). This would inevitably mean overcrowding – there's little enough room in a small cabin boat anyway – and after you've stepped on junior a couple of times while leaving your bunk in a hurry to deal with some real or fancied emergency (is the anchor dragging?) there is apt to be a certain amount of bad temper on board.

The maxim 'a place for everything' must also, where small boats are concerned, mean 'a place for every*one*'.

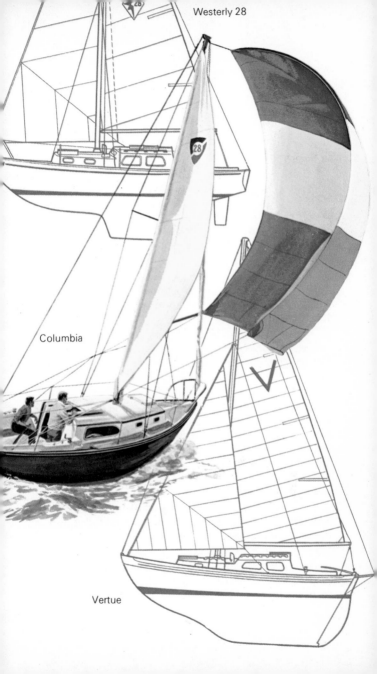

Westerly 28

Columbia

Vertue

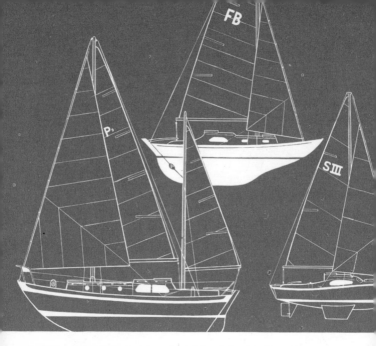

More cruisers : the ketch on the left is a Falmouth Pilot. Above is a Folkboat, and on the right a Silhouette Mark III. (*On the opposite page*) a Lark ; a South Coast One Design (SCOD) and an Atalanta.

More about cabin boats

An important point to bear in mind when buying a second-hand boat is that her accommodation is likely to depend on her age rather than her size; the older she is, the fewer berths she is likely to have.

Choosing a new boat

If you are in the lucky position of being able to buy a new boat of the size you need without too much regard for expense, a very wide field is open to you – a glance at the advertisements in the yachting magazines will show you what a vast number of designs there are on the market nowadays. Your only problem then will be to decide which to have. Do you want a boat with a glass fibre hull, for ease of maintenance? Or one with bilge keels, so that you can put her aground if you want to, or sit up straight if you do it by accident? Do you want one with a petrol engine or a diesel? (Diesel engines are more reliable, but more expensive.) Do you feel you can run to a boat with one more berth than you actually need? (This can be a great convenience, not only to accommodate the occasional guest, but also to enable you to spread yourself a bit.)

Standard designs
Cabin boats are not cheap, and it is unlikely that you will buy one 'blind'. How can you find out which will suit you best? You can, of course, learn a good deal from the yachting press, and pick up a good deal more from sailing acquaintances, and by visiting boatyards.

A very good rule of thumb here is to choose a boat of a tried and tested design. Find out how many of them have been built to date, and what sort of sailing the design is best suited to. If you then buy a new or reasonably recent second-hand one – after a survey – you are not likely to go far wrong.

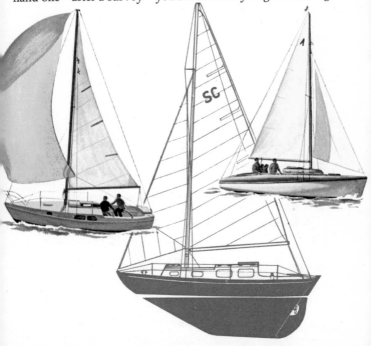

READY TO CRUISE

When you set off for a sail, you must be sure that your boat's hull, spars, rigging and sails, steering gear and ground tackle, (and her engine, if she has one) are in good order. If you are setting off on a cruise, certain other essentials must be aboard and in a satisfactory condition.

You will need a chart (or charts), a tide table, books of reference such as a nautical almanac, and at least one compass. You will also need navigation lights, and some means of checking the depth of water at any given spot.

Lights

The lights carried by various kinds of vessels will also be detailed later. Suffice it to say here that a small boat under sail should carry two navigation lights, a green one showing to starboard, and a red one showing to port. These may be positioned amidships – on the sides of the cabin top or, in some older boats, on the shrouds – or they may take the form of a combined lantern at the bow of the boat. The source of the light may be oil or electricity.

Lights are not required by law for boats of under a certain size, but obviously it is elementary common sense to carry them. For the same reason, a boat at anchor should have a *riding light*. This is white and may be a masthead light (electric), or a lantern (usually oil) hung up in the forepart of the boat, usually on the forestay.

Checking the depth of water

This may be done with a 'lead and line', which is simply a

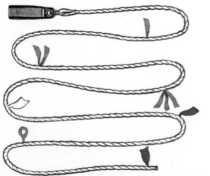

Lead and line: the line is marked at 1, 2 and 3 fathoms with 1, 2 and 3 strips of leather, at 5 with a piece of white cloth, at 7 with a piece of red cloth, at 10 with a piece of leather with a hole in it and at 13 with a strip of blue cloth.

length of line, with a lead weight at the end, which is marked in a distinctive fashion at various intervals to show how much line has been let out. Alternatively, some small boats now carry electronic echo-sounders. These are a great asset in that they show the depth at the touch of a switch, and are a particular boon in shallow waters, since they give a continuous recording of the depths under the boat's keel.

It is also useful to have a radar reflector, to indicate your position in fog, and/or a small foghorn.

Not only is it wise to carry this equipment; you should ensure that it is ready to hand and in working order. An echo-sounder is no use if its batteries have run down, nor is a radar reflector if you cannot find it.

(*Top*) an echo-sounder. Today many sailing craft carry this type of apparatus. It transmits an electrical impulse from a point on the hull to the sea-bed. The time taken for an 'echo' to return provides a simple basis for depth-measurement.
(*Centre*) radar reflector: a wooden hull will not register satisfactorily on a radar screen. This problem may be overcome by using a metal shape, hoisted to a suitably high part of the vessel.
(*Bottom*) riding lights, electric and oil.

Charts

Charts are maps of the sea. Coastal charts also show an outline of the land, and the principal features on the shore.

Charts, like land maps, come in various scales. They have a longitude scale along the top and bottom, and a latitude scale down the sides. The latitude scale can be used for measuring distances, because one minute (1') of latitude on the chart always equals one nautical mile.

Depths, directions and dangers

Charts give a great deal of information about the areas they cover. This includes the following:

The depth of water at any given spot is sometimes marked in fathoms (one fathom = 6 feet) and fractions of fathoms, sometimes in feet (the notation will be indicated on the chart); it is *the least depth which will normally occur there.* You will have to allow for the state of the tide to calculate the depth of water at any given time.

Sandbanks and the like *which protrude at low water* are always indicated in feet, and the figures are underlined thus: 6.

Navigational marks include buoys, lighthouses and lightships. Associated with these will be indications of hazards such as rocks, sandbanks and wrecks.

Compass roses, representations of the compass card superimposed on the chart, are used for navigating.

The direction and strength of **Tidal streams,** that is, currents in the sea, are marked on some charts.

The **Tidal range** is the difference in vertical height between high and low tide. It may be tabulated on the chart, together with other information which will help you to calculate the depth of water at any point at any given time.

Some charts have **Chartlets,** insets showing certain areas, such as harbours, in greater detail.

Some yachtsmen's charts also give special information on matters particular to sailing, such as courses to steer, anchorages suitable for small boats, and so on.

Section of a chart covering part of the waters between the Isle of Wight and the mainland of England (the Solent). Note the details.

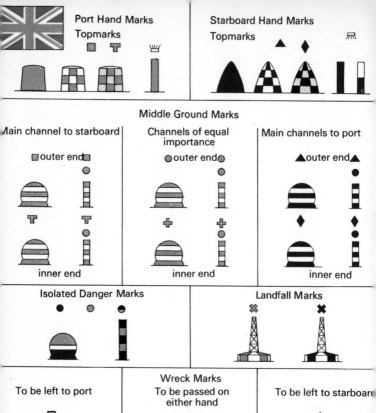

Port Hand Marks
Topmarks

Starboard Hand Marks
Topmarks

Middle Ground Marks

Main channel to starboard | Channels of equal importance | Main channels to port
outer end | outer end | outer end
inner end | inner end | inner end

Isolated Danger Marks

Landfall Marks

Wreck Marks

To be left to port | To be passed on either hand | To be left to starboard

Signposts of the sea

Buoys

Buoys mark dangers, such as rocks, sandbanks and wrecks, at sea and in rivers and lakes, and draw attention to such things as navigable channels. They can be identified according to their shape and colour, the topmarks that some of them carry for distant identification by day, the colour and kind of light that the more important ones exhibit at night, and

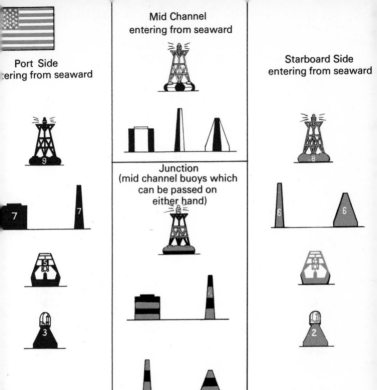

Port Side
entering from seaward

Mid Channel
entering from seaward

Starboard Side
entering from seaward

Junction
(mid channel buoys which
can be passed on
either hand)

the sound signals (bells, whistles, etc.) that a few of them carry as well. The light may be *fixed*, or *flashing* in a specified pattern, or *occulting* – shining most of the time but going out periodically.

Buoys are shown in miniature on charts, accompanied in some cases by notes on their special characteristics, if any.

Channel buoys (British system)
These mark the edges of navigable channels. They are strictly differentiated according to which side of the channel they mark *when a vessel is approaching harbour* (or moving in the same direction as the flood tide).

Lighthouses and lightships

Major hazards to navigation are marked by lighthouses and lightships. Each of these has a name, exhibits a distinctive light at night, and operates a similarly distinctive sound signal in 'thick' weather.

Lighthouses and lightships are marked on the chart in the same way as the more important buoys. Each is represented by a small symbol under which is printed the name of the lighthouse or lightship, the nature of the light displayed, and the characteristics of the sound signal. The height of the light above sea level will be given, and the distance at which it is visible in clear weather.

Lighthouses and lightships, being major signposts, are comparatively few in number. It is unlikely that there will be more than one or two (if any) in the average yachtsman's normal sailing area.

Local marks

At the other end of the signpost scale are the very minor marks found in rivers and inlets which are too small or shallow to be navigable by anything except small pleasure-

A British lightship. Note the distinctive colour and the prominently-displayed name.

In Britain, minor channels are often marked by withies (branches of trees) stuck into the sand or mud on either side of a channel.

craft. These marks may not appear on the chart, and will not necessarily conform to the accepted buoyage system, and local knowledge may be needed to interpret them.

Minor channels of this kind in Britain's sailing areas are often marked by withies, which are simply branches of trees which have been stuck in the mud or sand on either hand, usually by local fishermen or yacht clubs.

N.B. The information given in these last four pages applies strictly to marks around the coast of Great Britain. Other countries have different pilotage systems. In some large countries, such as the USA, the system may vary in different areas. Publications can easily be obtained giving all the necessary information for any given country or area. The variations may be considerable, so make sure you know them.

Warning!
Never risk a collision with a regular buoy of any kind. It may look small and harmless from a distance, but it is in fact a formidable, iron-clad monster. If your boat hits one, it will be the boat that gets the worst of it!

Compasses

Compasses are used at sea to find the way, and to 'fix' a boat's position. Although the same type of compass is used for both purposes, it is called a *steering* compass in the first case and a *bearing* compass in the second.

The basic function of a compass is to indicate the direction of north. The compasses used in large vessels are power-operated and indicate 'true' north. Those used in small craft work by magnetic attraction; they indicate magnetic north, and are called magnetic compasses.

Magnetic Compass

The magnetic compass consists essentially of a needle which points to magnetic north with, attached to it, a card indicating other directions with reference to magnetic north. The card floats in a bowl of liquid so that it can turn freely, and the bowl itself is suspended in such a way that it remains level whatever the motion of the boat.

Steering Compass

The compass used to steer by must indicate not only the direction of north, but also the direction in which the boat is pointing. The latter is known as the 'ship's head'.

The ship's head is usually represented by the 'lubber line', which is painted on the inside of the compass bowl.

Since the lubber line represents the direction in which the boat is heading, a steering compass must always be installed or shipped in a prescribed position. The compass card is the helmsman's static reference to direction. For example, if he wishes to steer south (180°), he alters course until the lubber line on the compass bowl lines up with south, or 180°, on the compass card.

Compass card

The compass card has directions marked around its circumference. The normal compass card has two sets of markings:

(1) The circumference of the card is divided into thirty-two segments or **points** (north, north east, north by east, north north east, etc.).

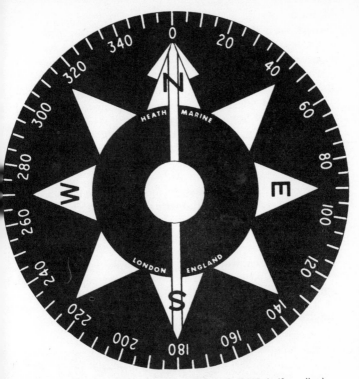

Compass card, showing the cardinal points (N, S, E, W), half-cardinal points (NE, SE, SW, NW) and the 360° system of notation round the circumference.

(2) The circumference of the card is also marked clockwise in **degrees**. This is the simpler of the two systems.

Compass deviation

Because a magnetic compass is basically a magnetized needle which is free to point towards anything that attracts it, it may be deflected from magnetic north by local influences such as iron and steel components of the boat, and also by certain kinds of electrical equipment. This angle-of-error may also vary with the course steered. If a compass has been properly sited, however, the deviation will never be large.

Navigation

Navigation is the technique of finding one's way from one point to another, making the best use of tides, avoiding hazards, and so on.

There are two kinds of navigation, deep-sea and coastal; the latter is more properly called pilotage. Deep-sea navigation is called celestial navigation because it involves taking observations of heavenly bodies (the sun, etc.). It is outside the scope of this book, for comparatively few small-boat sailors ever venture far from land.

Coastal Navigation : instruments

The basic instruments required for coastal navigation are a parallel ruler, dividers, a steering compass and a bearing compass.

Books and Tables

The coastal sailor will also require information on tides and tidal streams. Tide tables can be bought separately and information about tidal streams is sometimes given on charts

Use of the parallel ruler : a chart table, or suitable flat surface, is essential.

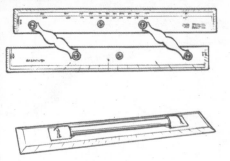

Some navigational instruments: the illustration shows two types of parallel ruler – the one above is 'walked' while the one below is rolled across the chart. (*On the right*) a pair of dividers (for taking off and measuring distances).

(see page 91). A nautical almanac is a comprehensive source of nautical information.

He will also, if he is wise, provide himself with a 'Pilot' of the area in which he is sailing. 'Pilots' are books, each of which gives details of a particular area, including hazards, navigational marks, courses, profiles of the coastline from seaward and other relevant information.

The Admiralty publishes a set of 'Pilots' covering all the coasts of the world. There are also special yachtsmen's 'Pilots' for certain coastal areas around Britain.

The small-boat navigator will also need a chart or charts and a chart table, which is simply a flat surface on which to lay out the chart. In a fair-sized boat – say a five-tonner – there may be room for a more or less permanent chart table. In smaller craft it will probably be portable.

A chart of the area in which you are sailing is a most important part of your navigational equipment, and it is vital that you use the right one for the job. A small-scale chart of a large area will be much less suitable for a short coastal passage than a yachtsman's chart of the actual waters you are sailing. Also, because sandbanks shift and sea-marks are moved or removed from time to time, charts become out of date. Corrections are issued periodically and may be made on the chart to update it, but the beginner's best policy is to buy a new chart or charts each season.

Section of a chart, showing a compass rose. (*Below*) how a direction is transferred from a compass rose to the required position on the chart.

Finding the course to steer

Working out the course to steer from one point to another is called 'laying off a course'. To do this you will need a chart of the area and a parallel ruler.

Parallel ruler

A parallel ruler is used in conjunction with a compass rose for transferring directions. It is so designed that it can be

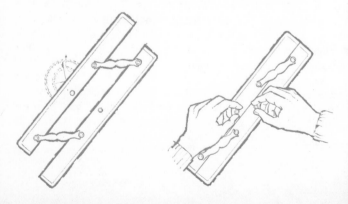

moved from one part of the chart to another without altering its 'lie'.

There are two main kinds, the bar type, which is 'walked', and the roller type, which is rolled, across the chart.

Compass rose
This is a representation of the compass card on the chart; on the average chart there will be several.

Laying off a course
Suppose your boat is at point A, and you want to find the course to steer to reach point B. Draw a line on the chart joining points A and B. Look for the nearest compass rose. Place the edge of the parallel ruler which is further from this compass rose exactly along the line you have drawn. Carefully 'walk' or roll the ruler across the chart until the edge which is nearer the compass rose passes exactly through its centre. Note the point at which that edge of the ruler cuts the circumference of the compass rose (in the direction in which you want to go). The reading at this point gives you the course to steer.

Practical check
Choose two navigational marks that are visible from each other. Lay off the course from the first mark to the second. Sail up to the first mark and put your boat on the course you laid off. The second mark should be dead ahead.

N.B. Other influences such as tide and leeway may have to be allowed for when determining a course. For the sake of simplicity these have not been taken into account here.

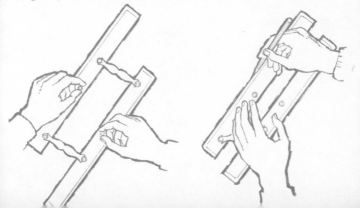

Taking bearings

Bearings are taken with a compass. The procedure involves sighting an object across the compass bowl. If the boat's steering compass cannot be used for this, a hand bearing compass will have to be used.

Hand bearing compass

A hand bearing compass is a small magnetic compass with a vertical, spigot-type handle underneath it which houses an electric battery for illuminating the compass card at night. There is an engraved line on the inside of the bowl, like the lubber-line on a steering compass, and a glass prism on the rim above it which magnifies a section of the compass card and enables the notation on it to be read more easily.

To take a bearing of an object, the hand bearing compass is held up to the eye (with the glass prism at the furthest point away from the eye). There is a notch like that of a rifle backsight in the prism, and the object is sighted through this. A reading is then taken of the point at which the engraved line cuts the compass card. This reading is the bearing of the object sighted from the yacht.

The object of which the bearing is being taken must be identifiable on the chart. The next procedure is to transfer the bearing to the chart. To do this:

Lay a parallel ruler across the diameter of the compass rose nearest the object so that one edge cuts the circumference of the rose on the bearing you have taken.

Move the parallel ruler across the chart until its nearer edge cuts through the object.

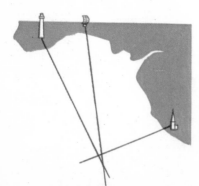

Fixing a position by taking bearings of three conspicuous objects. The triangle formed by their intersection is called a 'cocked hat'.

Taking a bearing with a hand bearing compass.

With the parallel ruler, draw a line from the object in the direction of your boat and extend it beyond the limits of your possible position.

This line is a *position line*. It is a representation on the chart of your line of sight of the object of which the bearing is taken, so your boat must be somewhere along that line.

Fixing a position

The procedure outlined so far will give you one component of a fix. If a bearing is now taken of another object which is visually identifiable and which is marked on the chart, and this bearing is transferred to the chart, you will then have two position lines. Your boat will then be somewhere along both these lines, and the only point where this is possible is where they intersect.

The second object of which a bearing is taken should be as nearly as possible at right angles to the first. Bearings cannot be taken with any great degree of accuracy from any

Fixing a position. The illustration above shows a sailing craft's position relative to the coastline and certain prominent landmarks. (*Opposite*) this position plotted on a chart of the area.

boat, and especially from a small boat in a seaway, and the greatest possible angle of intersection is necessary to reduce the margin of error.

'Cocked hat'

If possible a check-bearing should be taken of a third object. Because of the difficulty of taking bearings accurately, it is unlikely that the resultant third position line will pass through the point of intersection of the other two. Instead, a triangle known as a 'cocked hat' will be formed. A small cocked hat will indicate that your bearings have been reasonably accurate.

Running fix

This is a means of fixing your position by taking two bearings of the same object at different times. There are various ways of doing this, but the simplest involve 'doubling the angle on the bow'. To do this, you take a bearing of a suitable object and note how far you have travelled when this angle has doubled. The distance away from the object at the second position will be equal to the distance run.

A very convenient form of the above is to note when an

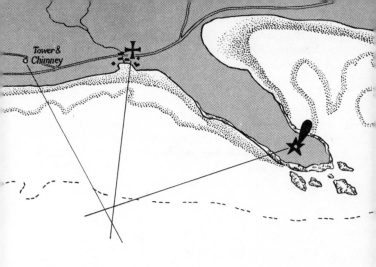

object bears 45° and then again when it bears 90°. The distance of the object abeam will then be equal to the distance run.

To take a running fix, the boat must maintain a straight course between bearings. Means must be available for judging the distance run, and allowance must be made for the possible effects of tides, currents and leeway.

When taking bearings, it is vital to be absolutely sure of the identity of the mark you are sighting. This may seem too obvious to be worth stating, but in point of fact it is very easy to mistake one mark for another. The golden rule here, therefore, is to choose the largest and most individual object that you can.

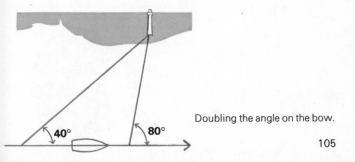

Doubling the angle on the bow.

Weather and weather-forecasting

Although the meteorological information put out over the radio and by various telephone weather services is invaluable, you should be able to make your own local forecasts too.

Barometer

This time-honoured instrument will always roughly indicate weather changes. The basic 'forecasts' it gives are simple and easy to remember. A high reading means fine weather and a low reading bad weather. A slow rise means less wind and rain, a slow fall the reverse.

Clouds

A great deal can be learned from the look of the sky, and in particular from clouds. There are four basic kinds of cloud: *cumulus, nimbus, stratus* and *cirrus*.

Cumulus is a 'piled-up' cloud, formed by rising currents of air. The small, well-separated cumulus clouds which look like balls of cotton wool are a characteristic of fine weather. If they increase in size, the air currents are becoming more pronounced, and the weather is on the change.

Nimbus is the typical rain-cloud – grey, and shapeless.

Stratus is a 'sheet' cloud. If it spreads over the sky, there will probably be rain, and the rain may last for some time, though it is unlikely to be heavy.

Cirrus is the high, wispy type of cloud which is sometimes called 'mares' tails'. Cirrus is an indication of wind, and if it spreads across the sky and becomes more regular in appearance, bad weather may be expected.

Weather

Strato-cumulus is a sheet of 'miniature' cumulus. If it spreads to cover the sky, wind is coming.

Yacht's barometer.

cumulus

strato-cumulus

nimbus

cumulo-nimbus

stratus

alto-cumulus

alto-stratus

cirrus

cirro-stratus

cirro-cumulus

Cumulo-nimbus is squally cloud, and consists of large, towering masses, very dark at the bottom. It is associated with heavy rain, violent gusts of wind and thunderstorms.

Alto-cumulus, as the first part of its name indicates, is high cumulus. The sky appears to be rippled with cloud. It is an indication of fine weather.

Cirro-stratus is thin cloud – it looks like a white veil. If it becomes more regular and pronounced in formation, the weather is probably going to deteriorate.

Cirro-cumulus is what is sometimes called a 'mackerel' sky. Small patches of it may occur in fine weather. If it spreads and becomes more regular in formation, the weather is probably breaking up.

As the above suggest, recognizing the significance of *changes* in cloud formation is the important thing – after all, we know what sort of weather we are having at any given time. Being able to forecast the weather that is coming and taking the appropriate course of action in the light of this is what really matters to the small-boat sailor.

Beaufort Scale

Forecasts of the strength of the wind are obviously of prime importance when sailing, and some scale of measurement is necessary. Winds are therefore measured by the *Beaufort Scale*, which divides the whole range of wind-strengths into 'forces' (every sailing man must have heard forecasts in which winds of 'Force 5' etc. are mentioned).

Knowing what wind strengths you can sail in is largely a matter of experience. It also depends on the waters in which you are sailing. A dinghy, for example, can sail on a river in wind strengths which might cause difficulties for her at sea.

Beaufort Scale

Force	Wind Speed (m.p.h.)	Sea Conditions	Inland Conditions
0	Under 1	*Calm* No ripples on surface. Any swell is not caused by wind.	*Light* Smoke rises vertically.
1	1–3	*Light Air* Patches of ripples on surface.	*Light* Smoke drifts. Stirring of flags.
2	4–7	*Light Breeze* Surface covered by ripples and waves up to 12 inches.	*Light* Wind can be felt on face, rustles leaves and moves flags.
3	8–12	*Gentle Breeze* Small waves 2–3 feet high, and occasional white horses.	*Gentle* Continuous movement of leaves, twigs and flags.
4	13–18	*Moderate Breeze* Waves increase to 4–5 feet and white horses are common.	*Moderate* Dust and paper blown about. Smaller branches swayed.
5	19–24	*Fresh Breeze* Crested waves 6–8 feet. Spray blown from crests.	*Fresh* Small trees sway about. Waves with crests formed on inland waters.
6	25–31	*Strong Breeze* Waves of 8–12 feet with spray streaks and crests foaming.	*Strong* Large branches swayed. Humming in telephone wires.
7	32–38	*Moderate Gale* White foaming crests to waves of 12–16 feet broken away in gusts.	*Strong* Large trees swayed. Difficulty in walking against wind.
8	39–46	*Fresh Gale* Sea rough and disturbed. Waves 20–25 feet, with 'boiling' patches.	*Gale* Branches snapped off, small trees blow down. Extreme difficulty in walking against wind.
9	47–54	*Strong Gale* Sea covered in white foam, waves 25–30 feet. Visibility reduced by spray.	*Gale* Chimneys and slates blown down.
10	55–63	*Whole Gale* 30–40 foot waves. Visibility badly affected.	*Whole Gale* Large trees uprooted. Buildings damaged or blown down.
11	64–72	*Storm* Air full of spray. Large vessels may be damaged by waves of 45 feet.	ditto
12	73–82	*Hurricane* Waves over 45 feet will damage large ships and may cause small craft to founder.	ditto

Simple passage-making

A 'passage', in sailing, simply means a trip from one point to another. In the case of the craft with which this book is concerned, and the experience and competence of the people sailing in them, this will usually mean a coastal passage. A coastal passage will normally involve pilotage by visual marks. It will necessitate the ability to read a chart and to identify buoys and other marks, and some knowledge of tides and tidal streams. A compass should be carried. This may not seem necessary if there are plenty of buoys in the area, but it may well enable you to find your way from one such mark to another should the weather become 'thick'.

Logs

A 'log' can mean one of two things in sailing. It may refer to a mechanical device which indicates how far the boat has sailed. This device consists essentially of a small propeller-like rotator towed on a line behind the boat, which, as it turns, registers on a dial on the boat the distance run. This type of log is not normally carried by very small boats on short passages.

End of a passage: this sloop is proceeding from right to left. At first she is under working rig. Roughly half-way, she has to shorten sail. Later, she lowers both sails and enters harbour on her engine.

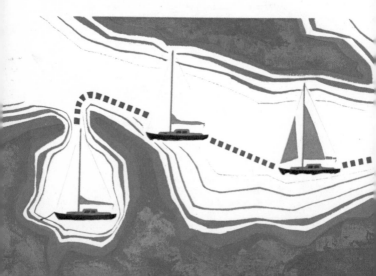

The other kind of log is a record of the passage, and should be written up regularly throughout the trip. Log books of various degrees of complexity can be obtained, but the simplest is the best for our purposes. In the log should be entered such details as the distance sailed, the course, wind direction and force, and the barometer reading. Provision is made for recording such entries hourly, and there is also space for your notes and comments.

It is not essential to keep a log of this kind, and many people do not bother to do so. It is a good practice, however, because it makes for an orderly passage – and it also provides you with a record of the trip.

It is easy to be frightened by a log book, and perhaps keeping one properly may seem a formidable undertaking. But buy one, even if to start with you only enter such details as where you went on the trip, who was aboard, and anything of note that happened. You may find yourself filling in the other columns before long.

On a passage of any length, a watch-keeping system should be organized. In other words, everyone aboard who is in any way competent to do so should take a turn at the helm. It is only too common for an owner with an inexperienced 'crew' to sail the boat virtually the whole way himself. But others on board will get much more enjoyment out of being in charge for a while, when everything is straightforward, and the skipper will be fresher for any emergency.

The illustrations on this and the opposite page show an anchorage (*left*) at high water, and (*right*) at low water. When deciding where to lie in an unfamiliar anchorage, make sure you will have sufficient depth at low water, unless you are prepared to go aground.

Simple passage-making (*continued*)

When making a passage, even a short one, the preparatory work is most important. This should involve not only such obvious aspects as provisioning the boat, making sure that everyone on board is adequately provided with warm and wet-weather clothing, lifejackets, and so on, but also a survey of the actual passage itself. A good rule is: always make your passage on paper before you set out, which means, in effect, 'sailing' the passage on the chart.

You should also decide, in advance, your time of departure with reference to the tide. The tide is important for two reasons. Firstly, a high or rising tide at the right stage of your trip may enable you to take a short cut across a shoal patch. Note, however, that you should never cut across such a patch on a falling tide unless you have plenty of depth in hand. Going aground, even if the bottom is soft, is at best annoying and bad for morale; if you go aground on rock or a hard bottom it can of course be dangerous. It can also be dangerous on a soft bottom if you go aground in an exposed position. You will probably be immobilized for several hours,

and during that time conditions may deteriorate, perhaps alarmingly. If nothing worse happens, you may scare your crew, and you will certainly shake their confidence in you as a skipper. The composite result may be that they will not want to sail with you again.

Time and tide

However, this is an incidental consideration. The real importance of studying the tide is to use it to advantage to help you on your way. No experienced skipper will sail against the tide if he can sail with it, and the reason is just a matter of simple arithmetic. If your boat is sailing at five knots and you have a two-knot tide with you, you will be doing seven knots over the ground, whereas at five kots, with a two-knot tide against you, you will be doing only three knots over the ground, which means it will take you more than twice as long to cover the same distance.

You may find it desirable to 'work your tides' so that for example you use part of the ebb out of a river to catch the flood tide up another. To do this you will have to leave when the tide is right, not when you are ready. Too many people say 'we'll leave after breakfast' whatever the tide is doing. This is a landlubberly way of going on. It may not be easy to turn out at three o'clock in the morning because 'the tide's right', but it will pay off later!

The 'Rule of the Road' at Sea

Always remember that when two or more vessels are in proximity a collision situation may develop unless those in command of the vessels know the 'rule of the road'.

The 'Rules of the Road at Sea' are published in pamphlet form by Her Majesty's Stationery Office. It is not necessary for the small-boat sailor to know all these rules in detail, but he should have a general acquaintance with them, and should know those which particularly apply to him so well that acting on them will be second nature.

Here are a few of the basic principles involved.

Vessels approaching each other

When two vessels are approaching each other, either directly or obliquely, one will, according to the rules, have precedence over the other. The one which does not have precedence must if necessary take avoiding action. But it is equally essential that the one that has precedence shall 'stand on' – that is, she should maintain her course and speed, so that the other chap knows what he is avoiding!

When two vessels are approaching each other head on, each must if possible alter course to starboard. This situation

Two vessels meeting head-on each alter course to starboard.

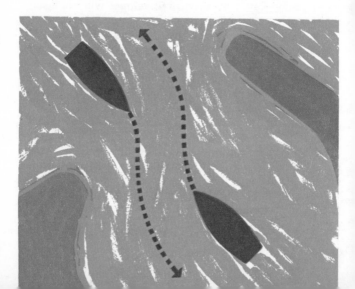

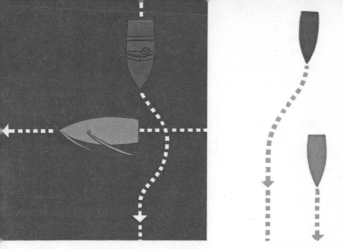

A vessel on the port tack keeps clear of one on the starboard tack. An overtaking vessel keeps clear of the vessel being overtaken.

will be encountered most frequently in narrow waters (rivers, for example), or entering or leaving harbour.

Power and sail
A vessel under power is normally required to keep clear of one under sail.

Overtaking
A vessel overtaking another shall keep clear of the vessel she is overtaking.

If you have to alter course, do it in plenty of time, so that the other fellow can see what you are doing.

The rules of the road must be interpreted sensibly. For example, a dinghy leaving harbour cannot expect a merchantman entering harbour to alter course for her.

Keep clear!
A good unofficial rule where large vessels is concerned is – keep out of the way.

The craft you are most likely to encounter are other sailing craft. Special rules governing these are given on pages 120–121.

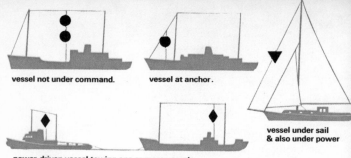

vessel not under command.

vessel at anchor.

vessel under sail & also under power

power-driven vessel towing one or more vessels, where length of tow exceeds 600'.

power-driven vessel towing one or more dracones.

'Shapes'

(N.B. This aspect of our subject is of interest only to those who sail on the sea, or in harbours, rivers and other waters where there is commercial traffic.)

It is necessary, when one vessel is in the vicinity of another, for each to know how big the other is, her means of propulsion, and also what she is doing (a commercial vessel may be doing many things other than simply proceeding from point A to point B).

By day, in clear weather, the first two of these particulars will be obvious enough, but the third may not be so easy to determine. For example, a vessel which appears to be approaching may in fact be at anchor; she may be towing one or more other craft; or she may be fishing. The small-boat sailor who does not know that a vessel is trawling and tries to sail under her stern will at best make himself pretty unpopular – and may well find himself in a very nasty predicament.

Particular activities or circumstances are indicated by visual symbols known as 'shapes'. These shapes are normally exhibited only by commercial craft. Small sailing vessels do not carry them because the activities they are engaged in do

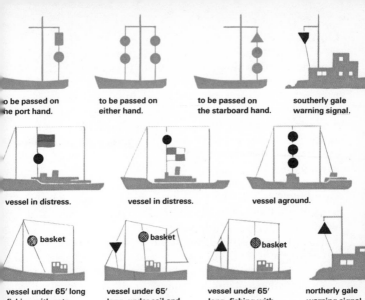

to be passed on the port hand.

to be passed on either hand.

to be passed on the starboard hand.

southerly gale warning signal.

vessel in distress.

vessel in distress.

vessel aground.

vessel under 65' long fishing with nets extending less than 500' horizontally into seaway.

vessel under 65' long, under sail and power, fishing with nets extending less than 500' horizontally into seaway.

vessel under 65' long, fishing with outlying gear extending more than 500' horizontally into seaway.

northerly gale warning signal.

vessel fishing with nets extending less than 500' horizontally.

vessel fishing with nets or lines extending more than 500' horizontally into seaway.

vessel laying or recovering a submarine cable or navigation mark.

not require them, and because such vessels do not constitute a serious hazard to others.

It may not be out of place to mention sound signals here. A short blast on a ship's siren is a warning to other craft that she is turning to starboard, two short blasts that she is turning to port, and three short blasts that she is going astern. In fog she will sound one long blast every two minutes when under way, two long blasts every two minutes when stopped, and a sequence of a short, a long and a short blast every minute when at anchor. Both power and sailing vessels sometimes use a bell for sound signals.

Lights

(N.B. As in the case of shapes, this section concerns only those who sail in waters where there is commercial traffic.)

By night as well as by day it is necessary for one craft to be aware of another's presence and position, and she must be able to identify her, at least as far as her size and motive power are concerned, and also as regards what she is doing. Indeed, identification is even more important by night than by day, for the consequences of collision are very much more serious.

This identification is established by means of lights, which are of two main kinds: (1) running lights, which indicate a vessel's kind and size; (2) additional lights, which indicate what she is doing.

There is one essential difference as regards (1), in that a vessel under power will carry a white light or lights at or near the masthead, whereas a sailing vessel does not.

The additional lights mentioned in (2) are equivalent to

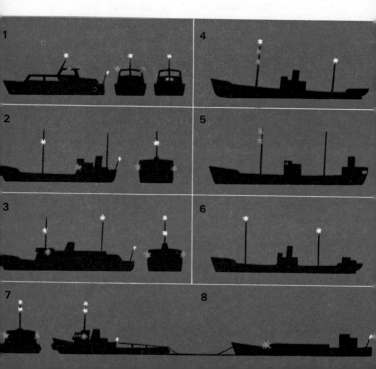

the shapes indicated on the previous two pages.

When under way at night a sailing craft should show a green light to starboard, a red light to port and a white light astern. At anchor, she should show a white light at a reasonable height above deck level.

Very small sailing craft, such as dinghies, are not required to exhibit navigation lights, but if there is any prospect of their sailing after dark they should carry a torch for use in collision situations. An ordinary electric torch, which may also be used for lighting one's way into narrow or crowded waters, is best for this purpose, and the best way of indicating the craft's presence is to shine the torch on the mainsail.

(1) power vessel under 20 tons. (2) power vessel under 150'. (3) power vessel over 150'. (4) vessel aground. (5) vessel not under command. (6) vessel at anchor. (7) vessel engaged in towing. (8) vessel in tow. (9) vessel engaged in underwater operations. (10) trawler under way. (11) fishing vessel under way. (12) seaplane under way. (13) auxiliary under power. (14) auxiliary under sail. (15) sailing vessel.

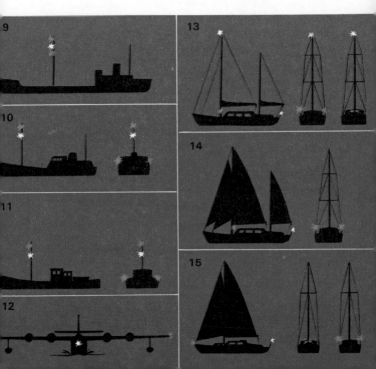

Rule 17

This is the most important of all the rules of the road at sea for the small-boat sailor, because it details the courses of action to be taken by sailing craft in collision situations.

Rule 17 states that:

(*a*) *When two sailing vessels are approaching one another so as to involve risk of collision, one of them shall keep out of the way of the other as follows:*

    (1) *When each has the wind on a different side, the vessel which has the wind on the port side shall keep out of the way of the other.*

    (2) *When both have the wind on the same side, the vessel which is to windward shall keep out of the way of the vessel which is to leeward.*

(*b*) *For the purposes of this rule, the windward side shall be deemed to be the side opposite to that on which the mainsail is carried . . .*

'Having the wind on the port side' means that the wind is blowing from the port side of the boat. It may be blowing from any point between bow and stern. A boat in this situation is said to be on the port tack. Similarly, in the case of a boat on the starboard tack, the wind may be coming from anywhere between bow and stern on the starboard side.

Another way, therefore, of expressing Rule 17 (1) is to say that in this situation the boat on the starboard tack has the right of way.

The expression 'to windward' in Rule 17 (2) means 'nearer to where the wind is coming from'. This regulation stems from the fact that the boat which is to leeward (further from where the wind is coming from) may in certain circumstances be in a less favourable position than the other, with less room to manoeuvre.

Another important rule affecting sailing craft is that a craft which is running free (sailing with the wind) shall keep out of the way of one which is close-hauled (sailing against the wind). This is because the former can manoeuvre more easily.

(*Opposite*) collision situations covered by Rule 17.

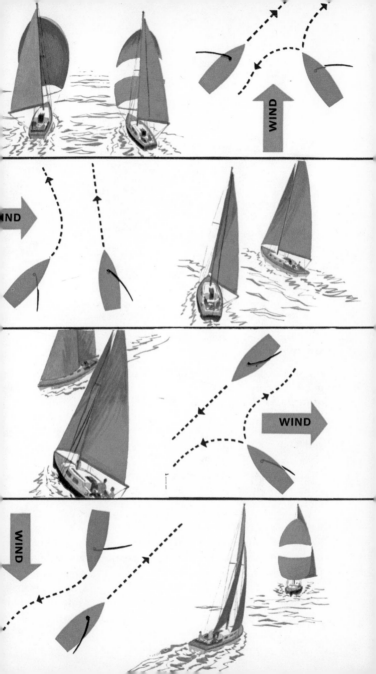

Safety at sea : an inflatable rubber dinghy is a much better lifeboat than a conventional dinghy. Flares can be of great assistance in indicating distress.

SAFETY AFLOAT

All small-boat sailors should keep one all-important thing in mind : *the water you sail on, whether it is the sea, a river, a lake or anything else, can drown you.*

There is no need to get neurotic about this, because that would spoil the fun. The best way is to observe all the rules and take all the precautions you can until safety afloat becomes a built-in instinct.

Safety afloat involves many considerations; some have been mentioned already, and others will be dealt with in more detail later.

Safety in dinghies

Safety in ship-to-shore dinghy tenders is *most* important. Never overload one of these little boats. If you do, a wave, perhaps from a passing power boat, may swamp her. On a dark night, with a strong ebb tide, this could easily result in tragedy. Also, when the tender comes alongside the parent boat, make sure that only one person stands up at a time while the others hold on, and that the dinghy's trim is preserved while the people in it transfer themselves one by one to the parent boat.

Safety in sailing dinghies is largely a matter of adequate buoyancy and of knowing what to do (and doing it) in the event of a capsize.

Safety in cabin boats

It is vital that a cabin boat be sound in all her parts and gear. Your engine, if you have one, must be reliable. You should take all possible precautions against that most terrifying of eventualities, fire at sea, and you should have the means of dealing with it if it breaks out (see pages 124–125). Whoever is in command must be sure that there are life-jackets for everyone, and that they are worn when necessary.

It is also important, especially where cabin boats are concerned, that there is someone aboard who is sufficiently experienced to undertake whatever kind of trip the boat is setting out on, and it should be clearly understood that he or she is in command, at least for the duration of that trip.

Safety afloat : when coming alongside, care should be taken in transferring to the parent vessel.

Fire at sea

If you are a dinghy sailor you do not have to worry about this particular hazard, but if you have a cabin boat, fire is a very real threat. Indeed, as we have said earlier, it can be the worst of all the dangers of small-boat sailing.

A fire can start very quickly, especially if it is ignited by an explosion. If it gets out of control, it may be necessary to abandon ship. The ordinary rigid dinghy tender will be of little use in such an eventuality, for it is easily swamped; this is another argument in favour of the inflatable type, which is much more seaworthy.

Explosion is attended by another hazard; someone – perhaps more than one person – may be injured or stunned by the explosion itself, and during the shock and confusion that follows the fire may spread disastrously.

Precautions

This presents a grim picture, but it is one that need never become reality, if you take a few sensible precautions.

If you have a **petrol engine**, you must make certain that the petrol tank does not leak, and that your fuel supply piping is in good condition and adequately secured at intervals, if necessary, and that any joints are sound. When filling the petrol tank, make sure you do not spill any fuel. *Always turn off the petrol at the tank when you switch off the engine.*

One of the advantages of having a **diesel engine** is that this hazard is not present, as diesel fuel is more difficult to ignite than petrol.

Most small-boat **cooking stoves** burn either paraffin or bottled gas. If you have a gas cylinder, you must again make sure that the fuel supply line is sound (and as short as possible). Also, *you should always turn the gas off at the cylinder after use.*

Many quite experienced small-boat sailors refuse to be 'shipmates' with any kind of bottled gas and prefer to cook by paraffin. This, however, is doing less than justice to the gas cooker, which is much more convenient than the paraffin type. If the simple precautions detailed above are observed, gas cookers are as safe as any.

Reserve fuel for the engine should be carried in as safe a

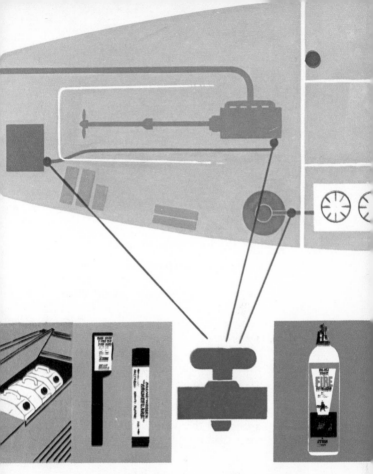

Beware of fire! All combustibles should be stowed in fire-safe places. There should be cocks to turn off fuel at the tank and the engine and, in the case of bottled gas, at the cylinder (*see diagram*). Also shown: a stowage for fuel cans, one type of fire extinguisher, and two kinds of flare.

place as possible (under the cockpit seats, for example, or aft against the transom; *not* below decks, and *not* near any possible source of flame, spark, or heat). You should carry at least one fire extinguisher, and keep it where it is accessible.

Falling overboard

Falling overboard is an ever-present hazard, and should be recognized as such.

The likelihood of this happening, as well as its consequences, vary considerably according to whether you are sailing in a dinghy or a larger boat. If you are in a dinghy, it is unlikely that you will 'fall overboard' in so many words, since when sailing in such a boat you don't – or shouldn't – stand up, which is when these accidents happen. In a dinghy, your immersion in the water is most likely to be the result of a capsize (see page 130).

When sailing in a larger boat, it is often necessary for members of the crew to work on deck from time to time, and it is mostly then that 'man overboard' accidents happen.

Guard rails

Any but the smallest cabin boat will, or should, have guard rails. These are literally an all-round protection, consisting of a rigid construction, known as a 'pulpit', round the bows, wires supported by stanchions rigged along each side, and perhaps another rigid railing (sometimes called a 'pushpit') round the stern. This latter is less commonly found than the pulpit, because there is little need to move about on this part of the boat when at sea, and in small boats anything that needs to be done aft can be done from the cockpit.

It is essential that your guard rails, if you have them, should be sufficiently high to be a real protection. On some boats they are so low that they are more like trip wires, and more dangerous than useful.

Safety harness

When *moving* about the deck, always hold on to something secure. There will probably be hand-rails along the cabin top. When *working* on deck, you may need to use both hands, and at such times, especially in a seaway, you should have some other means of attaching yourself. By far the best method is a safety harness, which consists essentially of a belt and shoulder-straps, and a length of line with one or more snap-hooks on it by means of which you can attach yourself to some suitable part of the boat.

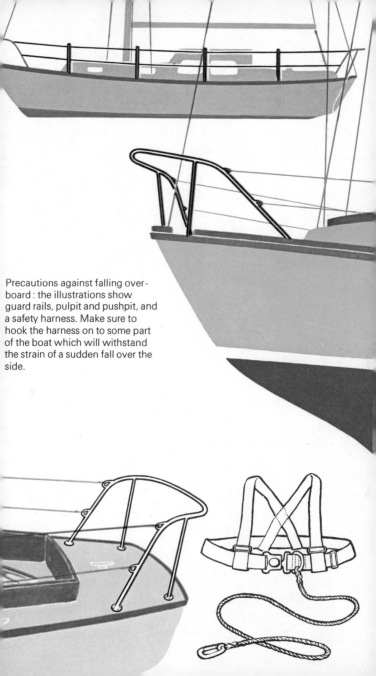

Precautions against falling overboard : the illustrations show guard rails, pulpit and pushpit, and a safety harness. Make sure to hook the harness on to some part of the boat which will withstand the strain of a sudden fall over the side.

Personal buoyancy : various types of buoyant jackets. (*Below*) buoyancy bags for dinghies. These must always be secured in such a way that they will not come adrift in the event of, say, a capsize.

Buoyancy equipment

Buoyancy equipment is of two main kinds – 'personal' buoyancy (life-jackets, lifebuoys, etc.), and 'boat' buoyancy (means by which the boat herself may be kept afloat if she becomes waterlogged).

Personal buoyancy

This is essential for all who sail, though some means of supporting the wearer in the water, which nowadays usually

means an inflatable or buoyant life-jacket of one kind or another, is of more immediate importance to the dinghy sailor than the cruising man, because of the ever-present danger of a capsize.

Stowage

In dinghy sailing, the stowage of life-jackets does not arise. In larger boats, they will probably be worn only when weather conditions require it, and stowed away at other times.

A number of points of great importance arise here: (1) there must be an efficient life-jacket, of the right size, for every person on board the boat; (2) these jackets must be stowed somewhere where they can be got at quickly and easily; (3) everyone must know where his particular life-jacket is stowed; (4) if the skipper decides that life-jackets are to be worn, his decision must not be questioned.

Boat buoyancy

This consists of either air-tight compartments built into the fabric of the boat, or, more commonly, inflatable bags which are normally held in place by straps. It is a feature of dinghies rather than cruising boats, since the former are more likely to fill with water (by swamping, or a capsize). Also, in most larger boats it is not possible to provide enough buoyancy to keep the boat afloat if she has filled.

N.B. There has been a great advance in personal buoyancy equipment in recent years and a wide range of jackets is now available.

(*Below*) two types of lifebuoy and lifebuoy stowage. They must be stowed in such a way that, while secure when not in use, they can be readily released. Always throw a lifebuoy near, not at, the person in the water.

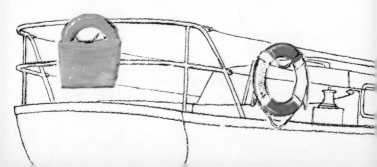

(1) two methods of righting a capsized dinghy; (2) how to get aboard a swamped dinghy; (3) baling out a swamped dinghy.

Man overboard!

The dinghy sailor is most likely to find himself in the water as the result of a capsize; the cabin-boat sailor as a result of falling overboard. The other essential difference is that, if a member of the crew falls off a cabin boat, the others aboard can at once begin rescue operations, whereas the dinghy will become a casualty herself. In this case, help must come from elsewhere – and it may take time.

Capsize drill

The golden rule here is *stay with the boat*. It is often possible for the crew of a dinghy to right a capsized boat unaided and continue sailing. If you can't do this, *stay with the boat and wait for help*.

Man overboard!

If you fall overboard from a cabin boat while sailing alone you will be in real trouble. So if you are alone you must take every precaution, especially when moving about.

If a member of the crew falls overboard, the following

drill must be followed without delay:

(1) Throw a lifebuoy, or something buoyant, as near the casualty as possible.

(2) Someone on board must keep him continually in view.

(3) If the boat is under sail, the helmsman *must gybe her*, whatever course she is on. This will turn the boat as quickly as possible and bring her into a position from which she can head back to the casualty.

Whether your boat is under power or sail, you should head into the prevailing conditions. If you do not, you may fail to slow down enough, and run the casualty down.

Three manoeuvres for picking up someone who has fallen overboard. The method chosen will depend upon wind and sea conditions.

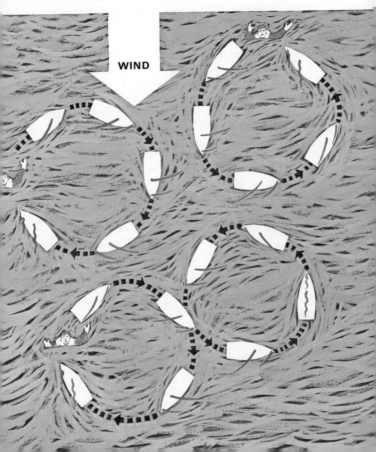

WIND

Night and bad weather

This section applies to cabin boats rather than to dinghies, since dinghies do not normally sail at night, and really bad weather is unlikely to affect them in that they will be near enough to their base to avoid it in the safest of all ways – by getting ashore.

As regards cabin boats, it is obvious that the worse the weather gets the greater the precautions that will have to be taken. What is perhaps not quite so apparent is that more precautions must be taken at night than during the day.

Mr. P. J. Haward, a very experienced yachtsman and the designer of a recognized and widely-used safety harness, says of such a harness that it should be used 'in bad weather, and *always* at night'. The importance of this will at once be realized if you think of someone falling overboard at night, and of how much more difficult it will be to pick him up in the dark.

Everyone on watch, therefore, including the helmsman, should wear a safety harness during the hours of darkness.

'On watch' brings up another point. On a night passage, arrangements should be made so that everyone gets some sleep. The crew should be divided up so that everyone except passengers or those not competent to do so takes a turn at sailing the boat. These watches should not be so long as to be tiring, and no inexperienced person should ever be left on watch alone. If any problems arise, the skipper should always be called if he is below, and he should give instructions to this effect.

Bad weather

The inexperienced should take every precaution they can to avoid worse weather than they feel they can cope with. Watch the weather forecasts. If possible, carry a radio and a barometer. Plan your passage so that you are unlikely to be caught in exposed waters, and can take shelter if necessary. Always reef in good time if a blow is coming. Extend your range only very gradually. Remember that if you get into trouble through trying to do more than you are capable of you may, if nothing worse happens, frighten off your friends or your family (and perhaps yourself) from sailing for life!

The risk of falling overboard is greatest when working on the foredeck — especially on a small craft without guard rails like this one. In these conditions a safety harness is not just useful — it is essential. Note that the line of the harness has two spring hooks enabling it to be used at different lengths.

THE SAILING YEAR

In Britain, a few hard-bitten characters sail all the year round, but for the majority the season afloat begins some time from March onwards and ends in September or October.

Fitting-out

This means getting ready for the new season. The amount and kind of work that will have to be done will depend upon the size and condition of the boat, and whether you can take her home or not.

Dinghies

Where dinghies are concerned, fitting-out is not normally a big job, since the boat itself is small and her gear light and simple, and also because, at least if she is a 'class' dinghy, she will have been kept in pretty well top condition anyway. A good deal of pre-season preparation for anyone who intends to race a 'class' dinghy will probably consist of making modifications of one kind or another to improve her performance.

Stepping a dinghy's mast. Most of the work entailed in fitting out a small boat can be done by the owner (and crew).

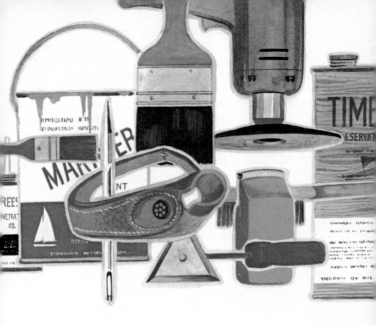

Some of the tools and materials used in fitting out.

Cruisers

Here the amount of work and its cost will depend very much upon the boat's size and condition, and upon the owner's competence (or that of his friends) to carry it out.

If the boat is trailed he can take her home and work on her at his convenience during the winter.

With a larger boat, it will be necessary to work on her *in situ* – in the boatyard or mudberth where she is kept for the winter. Most boatyards are quite happy for owners to do their own work on their premises.

You can have all, or some, of your fitting-out work done by the boatyard. The average yard will do a better job than the average yachtsman, but the fitting-out bill will go up accordingly.

You may feel sure that you cannot afford to have much done by the yard, but there is one respect in which you should spare no expense. This is in the doing of jobs beyond your competence (e.g. the renewal of standing rigging).

If you intend to have any work done by the boatyard, *do* give your instructions in good time. Most boatyards have only a limited labour force, and they always have a rush at the last minute – caused by boat owners who *have* left things until the last minute. If you are one of these you may find that your launching date is delayed, perhaps considerably – and that week or so when you hoped to be afloat but aren't is bound to be the best sailing weather of the year. As a result, you will be annoyed (with yourself, I trust), and so will the yard, much more justifiably, because of your lack of consideration.

Once you are afloat, make sure that your boat is ready in all respects for the coming season. Then do a short shake-down trip, to check that everything is in working order.

Mid-season maintenance

If you have fitted out properly, no major maintenance should be necessary. If any important defect does arise (damage to the pulpit for example, or the parting of a shroud as the result of a collision) this *must be put right before you sail again*. Never make do because 'it's nearly the end of the season', or anything like that.

Minor jobs which you can do yourself will almost certainly crop up. Do not put them off.

Engine maintenance should be a matter of routine. See that it is carried out regularly. So should such chores as washing down decks and the necessary 'housework' below. A regular routine should be followed here too. It is astonishing how dirty a boat can become, even on a mooring.

Scrubbing-off

A boat which is left afloat during the season will almost certainly collect weed and/or barnacles at some stage or other. This fouling will greatly reduce her speed, and a scrub plus a new coat of anti-fouling will be necessary. A boat with bilge keels can be beached at high tide for this to be done. A keel boat may be similarly beached or set up alongside a wall or the like, but in this case only one side at a time will be accessible. Some harbours and clubs have 'scrubbing posts' which boats can tie up to for this purpose.

A mid-season scrub may be necessary. For this the boat may be hauled out, or she may be laid alongside a wall, jetty or scrubbing posts. In the latter cases it may be hard going to get the job done before the tide comes back. Work may be done on the mast after it has been stepped by means of a bosun's chair.

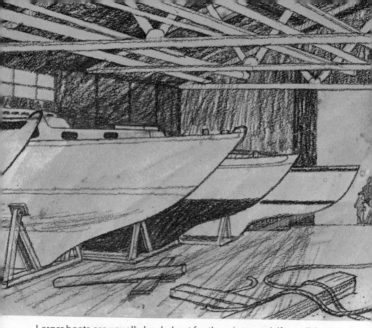

Larger boats are usually hauled out for the winter and, if possible, put under cover, as here.

All too soon the sailing season will be over, and your boat and her gear will have to be tucked away for the winter.

Laying-up

This procedure is known as laying-up, and the amount of work it involves will, again, depend upon the size and kind of boat you have. If you have a dinghy or a cruiser which you trail, the procedure will not be very different from that which you have been following throughout the season.

With a keelboat which you cannot take home, things will be rather different. You will need somewhere to 'park' her, and somewhere to stow her gear. You can take the latter home, if you like, or you can leave it in a local store, probably in a boatyard. The boat herself can be left in a boatyard, either outside, or under cover, if such a facility exists (the yard will haul the boat out and unship the mast, rigging and other equipment).

Mudberths

Some boats are left in mudberths. These are simply individual 'docks' along the high-water mark. The boat is floated in, secured on the top of the tide and left there. This method avoids the expense of hauling out, de-rigging and so on, and the boat will be reasonably accessible during the winter. But she will be more exposed to the weather than she would be if she were properly laid up ashore.

When a boat is laid up in the open, everything aboard her which is likely to be affected by damp must be removed. This includes bedding, and electrical equipment such as the magneto of the engine, if there is one. The engine should be properly immunized, and any batteries removed. The boat herself should be covered by a tarpaulin left open at the ends to permit the air to circulate. For the same reason all floor-boards should be lifted and all locker doors left open.

Now, too, is the time to look at your sails. Any repairs will probably have to be done by a sailmaker, since this is an expert's job. If you are lucky there will be a sailmaker at or near your base.

In point of fact, the sailing year never ends. There are many jobs you can do during the winter. If you have a cruising boat, you can brush up on your knowledge of the area in which you sail. Such study will be amply repaid when you go afloat again.

Sometimes boats are left in mudberths. A boat cover or tarpaulin is required, and the craft must be securely moored.

Taking her home

The boat trailer has affected the sport of sailing in two ways. Firstly, it has given many non-competitive sailors a choice of sailing grounds. Secondly, it has been a great spur to competitive sailing with dinghies by making it possible for dinghy sailors to take part in their own boats in regattas and meetings over a very wide area.

A boat trailer is basically a rigid metal framework with two or four wheels, which is attached to the back of a motor vehicle. This framework is equipped with padded supports for the hull, and arrangements for securing the boat to the trailer.

The most common type of trailer in use today is the two-wheeled dinghy trailer. These vary in design to a certain extent, but they are all lightweight and simple in construction. There is no 'loading' or 'unloading' equipment; the boat is lifted or floated on or off. Larger craft may necessitate the use of some type of four-wheel trailer. These are necessarily more complicated both in their construction and in their arrangements for loading and unloading the boat.

Since trailers are really road vehicles, they have to comply with stringent road regulations. For instance, they are subject to a speed limit, and they must have springs, inflatable tyres, mudguards, and rear lights. *Anyone who proposes to tow a boat of any kind on a trailer should familiarize himself with the appropriate road regulations.*

The relationship between the weight of the boat and trailer and the weight or engine capacity of the towing car is most important. Most modern cars will tow a dinghy with ease, but with larger craft the problem is not so simple. A car which is too light or under-engined may find itself being 'driven' by the momentum of its load; a car towing a trailer takes much longer to stop and overtake, and care must be taken to prevent the trailer from swaying across the road.

As a guide, the weight of the loaded trailer should not be more than two-thirds that of the car; or, alternatively, there should not be more than one hundredweight of boat for every 100 cc of engine.

A trailed boat means modifications to one's driving technique. So, on land as on water – take it easy at first.

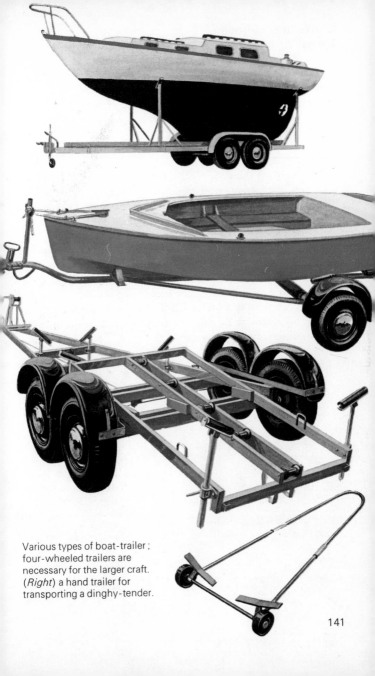

Various types of boat-trailer ;
four-wheeled trailers are
necessary for the larger craft.
(*Right*) a hand trailer for
transporting a dinghy-tender.

Knots and splices

The sailing man does not need nearly as extensive a knowledge of knots and splices as many people think. This is particularly true nowadays, when rigs and gear have been simplified and to some extent mechanized and when, instead of whipping or back-splicing it, the end of a Terylene rope can be prevented from fraying merely by applying the flame of a match to it.

However, it *is* still necessary to know the purposes for which certain knots are used, and how to tie them; how to make a loop on the end of a rope which will not slip (which will not, for example, if you are tending a swimmer, or helping him aboard, pull tight round his chest); how to join two ropes together (if, for example, you find you have not got a long enough warp).

The two main advantages of nautical knots and hitches are (1) they will not slip or come undone; (2) they are easy to untie.

The knots, hitches and splices illustrated on these pages are those the sailing man most commonly requires.

Some people like a bit of fancy rope-work on their boats. To discover how to do this, reference should be made to one of the books covering the subject.

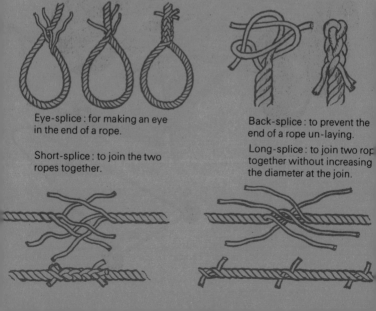

Eye-splice : for making an eye in the end of a rope.

Short-splice : to join the two ropes together.

Back-splice : to prevent the end of a rope un-laying.

Long-splice : to join two rop together without increasing the diameter at the join.

Knots, bends and hitches.

Reef-knot : for joining two ropes together.

Figure-of-eight-knot : a stop-knot, to prevent the rope running out through an eye, etc.

Clove hitch : for attaching a rope to a spar, stanchion, etc.

Rolling hitch : as above, with an extra turn for added security.

Bowline : for making a non-slip loop in the end of a rope.

Bowline-on-a-bight : for making two loops in the end of a line.

Sheet bend : for joining ropes of different diameters.

Sheep-shank : a method of temporarily shortening a rope.

Build her yourself

In part, the great increase in small-boat sailing during the past twenty years or so has been due to the production of kits for the amateur boat builder. In these kits all or some of the parts of the boat are prefabricated and supplied as separate units for the purchaser to assemble and finish. Since a very material part of the cost of any boat is the labour involved, this can mean a considerable reduction in your initial outlay.

Kinds of kit

Boats for home construction are supplied either as 'basic' kits, that is, those which leave the amateur builder to do virtually all the necessary assembly, or as boats at various stages of completion: for example as a completed hull which only needs 'additions', painting, varnishing and so on. Obviously the more constructional work the suppliers have done, the more expensive the kit will be – but the amount of work the purchaser will have to do will be less.

None of the popular kits requires any particular do-it-yourself skill, nor any tools other than the ordinary ones of amateur carpentry (the tricky bits, such as the centreboard case, may have been done for you). Most of the boats supplied in kit form are wooden ones, although in some cases glass fibre hulls are supplied for completion.

Plywood and glue

Two things have made amateur boat-building much easier and quicker than it used to be – marine plywood, and 'chemical' glue, which is used with a hardener. Most do-it-yourself boats are constructed of plywood, which means that some of the pieces supplied can be quite large – as large as one complete side of the hull, for instance.

And so long as the simple instructions provided are followed, chemical glue is easy to use and forms an exceptionally strong joint.

Most of the work involved in putting a boat together from a kit consists of fairing off the parts to fit, and screwing and gluing. And most of it can be done single-handed, though a little assistance will occasionally be needed.

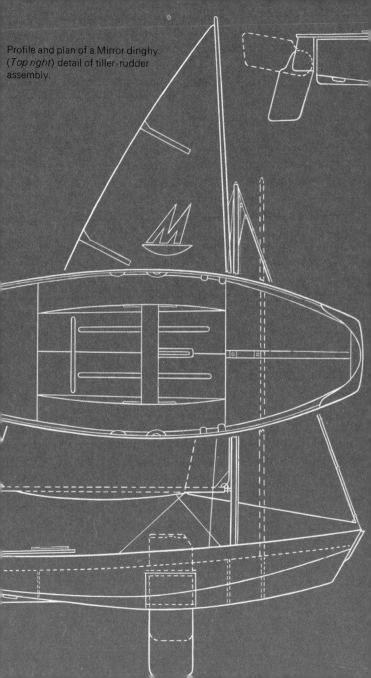

Profile and plan of a Mirror dinghy.
(*Top right*) detail of tiller-rudder
assembly.

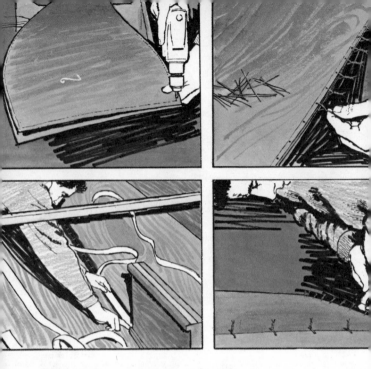

Build her yourself (*continued*)

The easiest kind of hull to build is a hard-chine hull with a pram bow. The Cadet has a hull of this kind, and so has the very popular Mirror dinghy. Both these boats can be bought either as a kit or as a hull with parts for finishing.

The illustrations on these and the previous two pages show stages in the building of a Mirror dinghy. Its construction is unusual in that a 'stitching' method is used to hold the major parts together in the first instance. The hull is made up of six of these parts, pre-cut. To assemble it, the pieces are held together and holes are drilled along the edges which are to be joined. These edges are then stitched together with short lengths of copper wire.

The next stage is to make the actual joint. This is done by covering the inside of the joint with the specially supplied resin and glass fibre strip, and, after snipping off the ends of the wire stitches, fairing off and repeating the resin and

146

Stages in the construction of a Mirror hull. (*Left to right, top*) drilling holes for the copper wire 'stitches'; putting in the stitches; painting with glue. (*Bottom*) fixing the glass-fibre strip; snipping off the stitches; the hull ready for painting.

glass fibre process on the outside.

When all these parts have been joined together and the hull is at the 'shell' stage, it will already look like a boat, but most of the work comes after this – the building and fitting of the centreboard and rudder assemblies, strengtheners, buoyancy compartments (if the design includes them), decks and deck fittings, the preparation and setting up of the spars and rigging, painting and varnishing. Patience and care are the most important requirements as far as the builder is concerned. If you have these qualities you will be amply rewarded. As some guide to how long it takes, the Mirror dinghy, which is 10' 10" long, involves on an average about 100 man-hours.

The damage resulting from even a minor collision may result in a big repair-bill.

Buying a boat

There are three main ways of buying a boat – by outright purchase, on hire-purchase, or on a mortgage.

Outright purchase is obviously the best and cheapest method. The majority of people, however, do not have 'that sort of money', and have to undertake some kind of deferred-terms agreement.

Hire-purchase agreements and mortgages

Mortgage terms are generally more favourable than those obtainable on a hire-purchase agreement. The rate of interest will be lower, the period over which repayments can be made can be longer.

In Britain, however, it is possible to obtain a mortgage only on a 'registered' craft, that is, one which has been officially surveyed and registered under the relevant clause of the Shipping Act currently in force.

If you are buying a new boat on deferred terms, the

finance company you decide to deal with will want the builder's invoice (and/or specification) as evidence of the value of the boat. In the case of second-hand boats an up-to-date survey report and statement of valuation are required on any boat costing more than £250.

The amount that a hire-purchase company will lend you on either kind of deferred-terms agreement will depend a great deal on the valuation of the craft. On a new boat or one in 'as-new' condition, you should be able to get a loan of up to four-fifths of the purchase price.

Insurance

Full comprehensive insurance must be taken out on any craft, whether new or second-hand, before it can be bought on deferred terms. The finance company will arrange this for you if you wish.

Insurance is not otherwise compulsory, but it is very foolish to go uninsured – as the cautionary pictures on these pages indicate. Even minor damage can mean expensive repairs, and premiums are not unduly high.

A boat may become stranded through dragging her anchor or breaking adrift from her mooring, or as a result of bad navigation or seamanship.

Chartering

Chartering is an excellent way of increasing your experience, and of familiarizing yourself with a larger boat than you could afford to buy, or would otherwise have the opportunity of sailing in.

Some charter firms and owners specify that their customers must be 'experienced'. Others merely ask the charterer to sign an indemnity which requires him to state his experience. Obviously, however, it is not wise for a group of complete novices to charter a boat, except in very sheltered waters.

Some charter firms will specify the limits of the area in which the charterer may sail. The charterer should be at pains to observe this restriction, for it will almost certainly be based on sound local knowledge.

Normally, the charter firm will provide everything necessary for sailing the boat and for living on board, and also life-jackets, and so on.

Chartering charges vary according to the part of the season for which the boat is chartered. A deposit will normally be required. At first sight the weekly rate may seem high, but it must be remembered that this sum is divisible among the persons chartering the boat; and that, from the charterer's point of view, sailing craft are expensive to provide and maintain.

It is normal for a charter party to go on board p.m. on a Saturday, and it should always be borne in mind that the charter is for a very specific period. The charter-cruise should be planned in such a way that the charterers are as certain as they can humanly be of getting back in good time. This is particularly important if the charter base is only accessible at certain stages of the tide. Missing the tide will mean a late return, with consequent disorganization for the charter firm, as well as disappointment and inconvenience for the next charter party.

Charterers should also always remember that they are 'on approval' in the sailing world. It is up to them to behave in as seamanlike a way as possible at all times.

(*Opposite*) a charter party going aboard.

Safety again

Here, for the sake of convenience, is a random check-list of points on this all-important subject. See if you can remember in each instance exactly what is involved. If you cannot, check back in the book.

Remember that water can drown you (or anyone else on board). Never attempt more than you are competent to do. Make sure that your boat is always sound in all respects, and that any important damage is repaired before sailing again.

Always reef in good time. Be careful about gybing. Always keep way on your boat, and make sure she carries some degree of weather helm. The tiller and the helm are your safety valves. In a dinghy, the mainsheet should normally be held, not secured. Always make going about a decisive manoeuvre. Make sure that the skipper *is* the skipper – and that everyone knows it. Always follow the correct procedure for hoisting and lowering sails, and for leaving and returning to a mooring.

An engine *must* be reliable, with sound fuel lines; and always follow a set procedure for turning fuel cocks on and off.

Dinghy sailors must always wear life-jackets.

Use a safety-harness when conditions warrant it.

Never overload a dinghy tender.

Make sure that everyone on board has a life-jacket and knows where to find it. Wear one when conditions demand it, and make sure that everyone else does (wear one all the time in dinghies). The same applies to safety harnesses. Never overload a dinghy tender.

Always veer sufficient cable when anchoring. At night, exhibit all the lights required for your vessel.

Learn all you need to know about navigating, *and* about the rule of the road at sea. Know your weather.

If you cannot right a capsized dinghy, stay with her until help comes. If you have a larger boat, know your man-overboard drill. If you sail a dinghy, both she and her crew must have positive buoyancy. Take extra precautions at night (what are they?).

No apology is made for this emphasis on safety. Sailing entails responsibility for not calling for help in an emergency which a little fore-thought could have prevented.

If you have thoroughly familiarized yourself with the foregoing, you should never have occasion to trouble the air-sea rescue service. And you will be helping to preserve the good name of the best sport in the world.

Carry a riding light when at anchor in an exposed place.

Always stay with a swamped or capsized dinghy.

Keep clear of large vessels.

Dinghies for fun ! This is how most people get the sailing bug . . .

Sailing sense

The prime satisfaction of sailing comes from pitting your wits against wind and water and using them to achieve some goal. Whether that goal is a trans-ocean passage or a quiet afternoon's sail is a matter of degree rather than kind. If you race you will have the additional satisfaction and excitement of competition against others, but the basic 'competition' will still be with the elements.

One or two final points may perhaps be made here before you put this book on the shelf and get under way:

Firstly: though the emphasis in the foregoing pages has been on safety, the intention has not been to alarm you, or to restrict you in any unreasonable way. *Do not do more than you know you can do* also means *do as much as you can do.* For instance, you may be sitting on a mooring on a fairly lively day, wondering whether you dare venture out into open water or not. The answer to this is, go out as far as it is safe and practicable for you to go, and have a look. If you have to come back, it doesn't matter, whereas to stay put,

154

... the wider horizons of cruising come later.

wondering whether you could have gone or not, is terribly demoralizing. It may end up with you rarely going anywhere at all.

Secondly: if you take your family or friends sailing, remember that they may not be as experienced or as confident as you are. You could frighten them off the sport for life. Remember, too, that sailing can be very dull for anyone who has not got anything active to do aboard (this applies particularly to children). So give everyone a turn at the tiller or a sheet to look after if it is feasible to do so. At the very least, *tell* the others where you are going, what is likely to happen at various stages, how long you estimate the trip will take. Then they will at least be able to take some intelligent interest in the proceedings.

Observance of the foregoing should greatly enhance your own enjoyment, and that of your 'crew'.

Finally: serious mishaps afloat are rare. You will be (or should be) much safer on board your craft than on the roads.

Good sailing!

BOOKS TO READ

SAILING

The Arrow Book of Sailing by Maurice Griffiths. Arrow Paperback.
Know The Game Sailing. Educational Productions.
Sailing by P. Heaton. Penguin Books.
Sailing Dinghies by J. Fisher. Bosun Books.
Starting To Sail by D. Cobb. Yachting World.
Starting To Sail by J. Fisher. Bosun Books.
Starting To Cruise by Guy Cole. Bosun Books.

SEAMANSHIP AND NAVIGATION

The Collision Regulations. H.M.S.O.
Safety in Small Craft by D. A. Rayner. Adlard Coles.
Knots, Ties And Splices by Burgess & Irving. Routledge & Kegan Paul.
Coastwise Navigation by G. G. Watkins. Kandy Publications.

GENERAL

Boat World (*Yearbook*). Business Dictionaries Ltd.
Reed's Nautical Almanack. Thomas Reed.
Buying A Boat by J. Teal. Temple Press.
A Dictionary of Sailing by F. H. Burgess. Penguin Books.
Fitting Out by J. D. Sleightholme. Adlard Coles.
Build Your Own Boat by P. W. Blandford. Stanley Paul.
Boatbuilding From Kits by Kenneth Mason. Bosun Books.
Weather For Yachtsmen by Capt. W. H. Watts. Adlard Coles.

To the foregoing may be added the various periodicals that are published on sailing. These journals are an important source of information on current trends in the sport, and their advertisement columns are an invaluable 'shop window' for anyone contemplating buying a boat, or equipment for a boat he already possesses.

ACKNOWLEDGMENTS

Charts on pp 90 and 100 by courtesy of Edward Stanford Ltd. Compass card on p 97 by courtesy of South Western Marine Factors Ltd.

INDEX

Page numbers in bold type
refer to illustrations

157

SOME OTHER TITLES IN THIS SERIES

Natural History

The Animal Kingdom
Australian Animals
Bird Behaviour
Birds of Prey
Fishes of the World
Fossil Man
A Guide to the Seashore

Life in the Sea
Mammals of the World
Natural History Collecting
The Plant Kingdom
Prehistoric Animals
Snakes of the World
Wild Cats

Gardening

Chrysanthemums
Garden Flowers

Garden Shrubs
Roses

Popular Science

Atomic Energy
Computers at Work
Electronics

Mathematics
Microscopes & Microscopic Life
The Weather

Arts

Architecture
Jewellery

Porcelain
Victoriana

General Information

Flags
Military Uniforms
Rockets & Missiles

Sailing Ships & Sailing Craft
Sea Fishing
Trains

Domestic Animals and Pets

Budgerigars
Cats
Dogs

Horses & Ponies
Pets for Children

Domestic Science

Flower Arranging

History & Mythology

Discovery of
  Africa
  North America
  The American West
  Japan

Myths & Legends of
  Ancient Egypt
  Ancient Greece
  The South Seas